MORALITY
WHAT'S IN IT FOR ME?

A Historical Introduction
to Ethics

MORALITY
WHAT'S IN IT FOR ME?

A Historical Introduction to Ethics

William N. Nelson
UNIVERSITY OF HOUSTON

Westview Press
BOULDER • SAN FRANCISCO • OXFORD

Copyright © 1991 by Westview Press, Inc.

Published in 1991 in the United States of America by Westview Press, Inc., 5500 Central Avenue, Boulder, Colorado 80301, and in the United Kingdom by Westview Press, 36 Lonsdale Road, Summertown, Oxford OX2 7EW

Library of Congress Cataloging-in-Publication Data
Nelson, William N.
    Morality, what's in it for me? : a historical introduction to
ethics / by William N. Nelson.
        p.   cm.
    Includes bibliographical references and index.
    ISBN 0-8133-7939-3 -- ISBN 0-8133-7940-7 (pbk.)
        1. Ethics. 2. Ethics--History. I. Title.
BJ993.N45   1991
170--dc20   90-42661
                                                                                  CIP

Printed and bound in the United States of America

The paper used in this publication meets the requirements of the American National Standard for Permanence of Paper for Printed Library Materials Z39.48-1984.

10 9 8 7 6 5 4 3 2 1

For
Barbara

CONTENTS

PREFACE

It is possible to read this book simply as an introduction to some of the major texts and ideas in the history of Western moral philosophy. It is not meant to be exhaustive, but it is meant to be accurate and, at the same time, accessible to readers with no previous training in philosophy. It grows out of many years of teaching historical introductions to ethics; one aim of these courses is just to provide an overview of a rich and varied philosophical tradition.

I hope the book is also something more. As readers with a philosophical background will see, it is written from a distinctive viewpoint that reflects my own philosophical preoccupations. These arise out of three convictions. The first, to which the book's title is meant to point, is a democratic conviction that moral demands, if they are worth our attention at all, must be defensible *to* those to whom they are addressed. Second, whether or not moral truth consists in correspondence to some independent reality--whether or not "moral realism" is true--the issue of urgent practical importance regarding any moral conception is whether people have reason to *care* about it so that it constitutes a consensus of concern to which the members of a community can effectively appeal in their dealings with one another. The third conviction consists of a broad, philosophical naturalism: The natural world, the world of the natural sciences, is the only world there is. Morality must find its place within this world. By putting these ideas together, then, I arrive at the conclusion that moral facts, if there are any, must be natural facts about people or the world they live in, and they must be facts that most of us have a reason to care about. Moral facts are natural facts, but they are natural facts that *matter*.

I should say a couple of words more about the first and second of these convictions. While I hold that moral demands must matter to people and must be defensible to those to whom they apply, I do not mean that they must be defensible in terms of individual *self-interest*. Indeed, one of my aims is to draw attention to some of the classic arguments against the thesis that we are necessarily self-interested, and I criticize the philosophers who think we are. In general, a defense of morality--a defense *to* those to whom it applies--forces us to look at two questions at once: "What does morality require?" and "what motives and interests do people normally have?" Without answers to both, we cannot carry out the project of justification. Our question must be whether there is some conception of morality and some plausible account of human motivation, such that persons motivated as that account says they are can also be expected to care about morality as it is conceived.

Because I reject the thesis that people are merely self-interested, the question in the title ("what's in it for me?") has a sort of double purpose. For parts of what has traditionally been studied under the title "ethics," it raises a hope that actually can be fulfilled, for these parts do contribute to one's own good. At the same time, it calls attention to the fact that other parts of morality cannot be so justified. For them, the answer to "what's in it for me?" is "not much." But that does not mean these aspects of morality cannot be defended at all. For, again, people are not merely self-interested. They are susceptible to moral considerations of various kinds. They are able to adopt the perspective of others and to care about what can be justified to them. And so, even when morality requires that we adopt an impartial standpoint, morality can still be justified, at least to most normal people.

In the course of examining a number of key historical texts, this book focuses on ideas about what morality is, what ethics is about. The ideas it examines range from the Greek notion that ethics is concerned with what an individual needs in order to flourish to Hume's idea that morality is concerned with the well-being of others and is rooted in natural capacities for sympathy and benevolence that lead us to share this concern. And, of course, it explores other ideas as well, most notably Kant's version of the idea that moral laws are laws of reason. It also explores various sophisticated, or not so sophisticated, ideas about human motivation.

Readers familiar with the philosophical literature will find, no doubt, that some of their favorite topics have been omitted. This is inevitable in any book, but I hope, in this one, that what is omitted is at least omitted for a reason. To take one example, though there is a chapter on Bentham and Mill, there is no discussion of the distinction between direct and indirect utilitarianism. That is because, from the perspective of this book, what is most striking about utilitarianism is something both the direct and indirect versions have in common--their aggregative, maximizing consequentialism. It is this feature of the theory, after all, which writers in the contractualist tradition attack even when the utilitarian principle is viewed, in the style of rule-utilitarianism, as a "principle for institutions."

Omitted also is any discussion of religiously based ethical theories. As important as these may be for the history of ideas, theology has no place in the philosophical naturalism that I presuppose. What I hope I have managed to include are the major historical alternatives in terms of which contemporary debates tend to be framed. For someone who wants to get a sense of the differences between Greek ethics and post-enlightenment ethics, of the Greek notion of the virtues, of the modern debates between Kantian and utilitarian theories, and of the way in which contractualist theories draw on both traditions, this is meant to be the book.

William N. Nelson

ACKNOWLEDGMENTS

In working on this book I have benefited from the advice and suggestions of many people. Early on, Howard Curzer and Cynthia Freeland read a draft of the first half and offered detailed comments and criticisms. Eugene Schlossberger and Nancy Snow read a revised and augmented version of the same material for Westview Press, and later Alan Ryan, David Schmidtz, and Henry West read and commented on the complete text. My daughter, Sarah, read sections, offered comments, and, when the title needed changing at a late date, made the suggestion that led to the final version. Spencer Carr of Westview Press read draft after draft, commenting, criticizing, and asking hard questions. It has been a great help that he knows both publishing and philosophy, but just as important for me has been his good cheer and sense of humor. It has been a pleasure to work with him. Needless to say, not all of these people agree with what I say or with how I say it, but each made suggestions that have improved the final version. I am grateful to all of them for their help. I am grateful, too, to Barry Brown, at the University of Houston, who helped immensely with the task of formatting the final text.

I owe another debt of a different kind to my family--my wife, Barbara, and my children, Andrew and Sarah. Much of what I have managed to learn about how to live my own life I have learned from them. They help make it the good life that it is.

W.N.N.

MORALITY
WHAT'S IN IT FOR ME?

A Historical Introduction
to Ethics

INTRODUCTION:
WHY BE MORAL?

"Why be moral?" is not the only question of moral philosophy; nor is it necessarily the most important. But it is a surprisingly good place to begin an introduction to moral philosophy. One reason is that there is no way to answer this question, or even to discuss it intelligently, without raising and investigating a number of other important issues in moral philosophy.

A second reason for starting with this question has to do with the contemporary cultural and political climate. We find ourselves confronted, both as individuals and as a community, with what seems like a much broader range of difficult choices than ever before. Some of these choices arise from things like advances in medical science that create opportunities never available in the past. Other choices result simply from cultural change--from the fact that people have come to consider as possibilities options that used to be ruled out without any thought.

We face many new and difficult choices, and many people see these as *moral* choices. There is no question in their minds that the *right* choice is the choice dictated by morality. And so we find ourselves bombarded on all sides by moral demands: We are told that abortion is immoral and must be outlawed, but also that women have absolute rights to make their own choices regarding abortion; that moribund lives must be preserved as long as technologically possible, and also that people have rights to "die with dignity." And we are told that capital punishment must be abolished, that the policy of nuclear deterrence is immoral, whether or not it works; and we are even told that it is immoral for women to be umpires in the major leagues.

Obviously, we cannot heed all of these demands. They are not even consistent. In the case of some, were we to heed them, the costs, both in financial terms and in terms of human happiness, might well be immense. Yet, once the term "moral" is attached to a demand, few people, at least in public and especially in political discourse, feel free to ignore the demand. No one wants to admit indifference to morality. If these are true moral demands, however, and if I am right in saying that what they require could be extremely costly in terms of human happiness, then it seems to me that the question "why be moral?" is a very important question indeed. Moreover, if the costs of being moral are high enough, the answer may be that there is no good reason to be moral. Perhaps, as philosophers like Friedrich Nietzsche have thought, morality is a disaster for anyone who cares about human well-being, not to mention his or her own well-being.

Most philosophers would object to this way of looking at the issue. They would agree that many of the *alleged* demands of morality are unreasonable, if not downright repressive. But they would say that I have chosen my examples unfairly. The rigid, inflexible, and repressive rules some people associate with morality are not genuine moral rules. The real requirements of morality do sometimes demand sacrifice, but not usually great sacrifice; and the sacrifices they do demand are in the service of liberal and humane ends. The *genuine* requirements of morality, most philosophers would say, are important because they protect and promote central human interests.

This sounds like a reasonable response. But notice what it means. It means that we cannot answer the first question I raised--"why be moral?"--without answering a second question, namely, "what kind of thing does morality require?" Perhaps it is true that the actual requirements of morality are important and reasonable and that the shrill exhortations of dogmatic moralists are based on mistaken conceptions of morality. But that remains to be shown. We have two questions to answer, not just one. And how is the second question to be answered? Many philosophers have thought that in order to understand what morality requires, we need to understand what morality *is*, that is, what it is about or what its point is. And that, of course, is a third question. (Just as an example, if the point of morality is to enable people to live together in peace and harmony, then morality actually requires whatever is required to produce peace and harmony.)

Indeed, there are really more questions than these. When we ask "why be moral?" we need, as I have just said, to think about what we are trying to justify. We also need to think about what kind of justification we have in mind. If we think the requirements of morality are important, the question remains, important for whom, and in what way? Questions like these represent a fourth kind of question. No doubt, different people would accept different answers. Some would be satisfied if they were shown that moral or ethical conduct serves the interests of others, or of society. But others find this kind of answer inadequate. Perhaps, like the inquisitor I imagine in the title of this book, they will want to know "what's in it for me?" As they see it, the fact that moral conduct serves the interests of others justifies morality only to someone who is already concerned about social good; and that, they would say, is itself an ethical commitment. How can morality be justified to someone who is not already moved by moral considerations?

Once again, the person who raises this question may have in mind more than one kind of answer. A particularly interesting kind of answer, however, and one that has aroused a good deal of interest in the history of philosophy, is that being moral, though it seems to require a concern for the good of others, also contributes to one's own well-being, one's own good, where this in turn means something like happiness. Some philosophers have thought that this idea must be wrong. After all, if we know anything about morality, we know that morality is meant to serve as a check on self-interest. Nevertheless, others remain convinced that one is better off being moral than not being moral, and that the demands of morality can be justified by appeal to this idea. To explore this line of thought in any depth, of course, we need to deal with yet another basic question, a fifth one, namely, "what kind of life is a good or happy life?"

I have raised so far a series of basic questions, including:

- Why be moral?
- What does morality actually require?
- What is the good life? (or what is human well-being?)
- What is morality about?
- What kind of answer to "why be moral?" is a good one?

If this book were meant to be a systematic treatise on moral philosophy, I would go on to explore possible answers to these questions and, perhaps, endeavor to show that there is at least some reasonable conception of what morality requires, and some corresponding reasonable conception of human well-being, in terms of which it is possible to show that being moral contributes to well-being (or is at least consistent with it). Indeed, in my final chapter, I will attempt to show this. But while I do aim to address substantive issues in moral philosophy, I also mean to write an introduction to the history of ethics. Rather than proceed directly to answer the questions I have raised, then, I will use them as a way of organizing my discussion of certain central works in the history of moral philosophy: As I approach the philosophers I discuss, my question will be how *they* would answer these questions. I hope to show both that the history of ethics makes more sense when approached with substantive issues in mind and also that a historical perspective contributes to our understanding of the substantive issues.

Of course, not all the philosophers I discuss will answer my questions in the same way. Not all of them even ask these questions. Indeed, it is one of my main themes that the Western tradition in moral philosophy is not a history of different philosophers investigating the same questions and coming up with different answers. Instead, in a quite clear sense, it is a history of different philosophers asking different questions and, not surprisingly, offering different answers. Moreover, even when the questions raised by different philosophers appear to be quite similar, it is often clear, on investigation, that the philosophers' understanding of what those questions meant, and what kind of answer would be appropriate, are quite different.

These differences should not be exaggerated. Even when different people have asked different questions, it often seems plausible to say that they are dealing with different aspects of the same underlying phenomenon; and it is also often true that the issues they address are complementary. That is, the answer one theorist offers to one question is clearly useful to others dealing with other issues. Still, what we find when we look at the history of ethics is something less than a coordinated effort to find answers to a single set of questions. Instead, we find disagreement not only about answers and procedures for finding answers but also about the questions themselves.

Disagreement about the questions themselves, I should point out, is characteristic of philosophy--and is often frustrating for students. In the more specialized sciences that have spun off from philosophy (like physics or biology), there is usually a good deal of agreement about what the basic questions are, and even about how to go about answering them. As sciences progress, more and more answers are discovered. For students, the job is to learn the answers, to learn why they are correct, and, for the more advanced, to learn how to discover more. Philosophers, though, whether they are engaged in pure philosophy, or in the philosophical study of a more specialized discipline, push their investigations further. And often that means questioning the questions themselves. Why should we be asking *this* question rather than *that*?

This means that studying philosophy is like a juggling act: You have to keep both answers and questions in the air at the same time. You frequently end up with a lot of "ifs." "If this is the question, then here is a possible answer, but if we ask a *different* question. . . ." That is one of the things that makes philosophy difficult, but it can also make it especially rewarding. Once you get the hang of it, it is liberating, for it means that you don't have to be stuck with someone else's conception of what the right questions and the right methods are. And the very best and most exciting work, in just about any field, has always come from those who had the ability to conceive of new ways of approaching an old subject. One of the great advantages of a historical approach to ethics is just that it provides us with such a variety of different approaches.

I began this introduction by drawing attention to an increasingly shrill, moralistic strain in public discourse, a moralism that is both self-righteous and dogmatic. One might think that, as a philosopher who specializes in ethics, I would applaud this development, but I do not. I would certainly like what I view as a moral or ethical outlook to become more prevalent. But I do not equate a belief in the importance of a moral outlook and rational moral discourse with a dogmatic commitment to any particular moral judgment regarding the kinds of issues we confront as a society. Dogmatism and objectivity are, in fact, incompatible. People like me, who believe that moral judgments can be objectively true or false, believe that the true ones are true only if they can be supported by good evidence. They think evidence needs to be examined, and reasons on both sides considered. Dogmatists believe what they believe without considering evidence and without being willing to reexamine what they think in light of the evidence. What believers in moral objectivity really care about is whatever is supported by the best evidence. They are prepared to accept the possibility that even what *they* think is correct *might* not be.

The philosophers I will discuss here are not dogmatists. All of them make an effort to provide some kind of systematic defense for their conclusions. None means merely to *assert* alleged moral truths, and none rests his conclusions merely on faith, or commitment, or religious conviction. But what kind of defense can one offer for a *moral* judgment? What kind of evidence is possible? The best way to answer this question is to refer the reader to the discussions, in the chapters that follow, of the particular arguments philosophers have offered. Many of them are good arguments that support their conclusions with the evidence of experience or with common sense observations about the facts of personal or social life. They may simply remind us, for example, of the things we have learned, as we grow, about what is or is not satisfying in our lives, and of what attitudes have caused us trouble. Some of the arguments we will discuss, however, are not so good. Like anyone else, philosophers make mistakes of reasoning. They leap to conclusions, they generalize too quickly from a small sample, or they overlook alternatives to the conclusion they favor. It will be my job to try to point out those errors. But even when there are errors, they are seldom silly errors. We can usually understand the philosophical temptations that lead to them, and we can learn not to repeat them ourselves.

Still, one might wonder just how any experience or any facts about life in society could, all by themselves, tell us what is right or wrong, good or bad. The answer is that they can't. What they show will depend partly on what *other* assumptions one is willing to make about the purpose of morality, about the nature of the basic questions of ethics. Thus, for example, if we think morality is something like a code of behavior whose function is to promote some goal, either for an individual or for society (just as rules for investing have the function of helping people to achieve success in the stock market), then it is clear how facts about human experience could be evidence for or against an ethical theory. It is also clear, on this assumption, that if a theory is a good theory, there ought also to be some interesting answers to the question "why be moral?" as morality is conceived in that theory.

The arguments of the philosophers I will discuss, then, like any arguments, rest on assumptions; and these philosophers, by the standards of the twentieth century, are relatively unaware of the extent to which they are making controversial assumptions. Or, at least, that is the way they naturally appear to us, for we may be aware of more alternatives. Assumptions these philosophers thought obvious, proofs they thought beyond question, often seem to us dubious. That is another reason why it is valuable to look at the history of philosophy. We are sufficiently distant from it that we can look at it objectively, critically. We can see the flaws and shortcomings. But the real payoff comes when, having become aware of these shortcomings, we ask ourselves whether *we* really have an improvement, whether *our* assumptions are any more firmly grounded. The answer, more often than not, is that they aren't. When we understand that, we may be in a better position to approach moral conflicts in a spirit of respect for the opinions of others and to think creatively about how to resolve them, free from the assumption that the answers have already been found and need only be forced upon those who disagree.

I will begin my discussion of moral philosophy with two representatives of the ancient Greek tradition. I will then take a giant leap to the seventeenth, eighteenth, and nineteenth centuries and discuss several philosophers from that period. Between these two periods, as I will explain, ideas about what morality is, what its point is, and what its requirements are, changed quite dramatically. The reason, I suspect, had a lot to do with the influence of the Judeo-Christian tradition--a tradition which obviously did not influence the early Greeks. In any case, within each period, though there are often significant disagreements among philosophers, there are also important similarities just beneath the surface.

Along with many others who have recently written on this history, I will take Aristotle to be the main representative of the Greek tradition, and I will discuss him at length in Chapter 2. I will start, though, not with Aristotle in the fourth century B.C., but with the Stoic philosopher Epictetus in the first century A.D. Not only are his views a great deal simpler and easier to expound than Aristotle's, but also his conception of the ethical life, it seems to me, contrasts far more sharply with modern ideas about morality. It seems like a good place to start, then, if we want to begin thinking about ethics in a new way.

PART ONE
The Greek Tradition

1

SELF-DISCIPLINE AND TRANQUILITY

EPICTETUS, A.D. 50-130

Do not seek to have events happen as you want them to, but instead want them to happen as they do happen, and your life will go well [s. 8].

So says Epictetus in the *Encheiridion*, or, in the translation I am using, the *Handbook*,[1] a collection of sayings and pieces of advice taken from the longer *Discourses*. The son of a Greek slave, born in Asia Minor in about A.D. 50, Epictetus was himself taken to Rome as a slave. Eventually freed but later banished from Rome by Emperor Domitian in A.D. 89 or 92, he lived as a teacher in Nicopolis, on the northwest coast of Greece, until his death in A.D. 130.

The saying I have quoted above is typical of much of what Epictetus says in the *Handbook*. Well-being, he insists, depends not necessarily on external events, which may or may not work out as we would like, but rather on the desires and attitudes we adopt. At the very beginning of the *Handbook*, Epictetus calls our attention to the fact that our powers are limited. "Some things are up to us and some are not up to us" [s. 1]. The things that we can control--that are up to us--are "our impulses, desires, [and] aversions." "Our bodies . . . possessions . . . reputations . . . public offices" are not up to us. If we wish to live well, what we must do is concentrate on the things that are in our control. If we seek possessions or reputation and do not get them, we will be disappointed and frustrated. But if we avoid such desires in the first place, we rule out the possibility of these disappointments.

That is at least part of Epictetus's point, and it seems to be what he has in mind in the first passage I quoted. Sometimes, though, his remarks seem to have a different emphasis. For example, he says that not only should we limit our desires, but we should also learn as much as possible about the actual nature of things and maintain an awareness of what we learn. Thus, he tells us, if you are fond of something, "remember what sort of thing it is." If it is a jug, remember that it is a jug, "for when it is broken you will not be upset." Jugs, after all, do break. And "if you kiss your child or your wife, say that you are kissing a human being; for when it dies you will not be upset" [s. 3]. Again, if you are going out to the public baths, "put before your mind what happens at baths--there are people who splash, people who jostle, people who are insulting, people who steal" [s. 4].

This second kind of advice, that we understand the nature of the world we live in, is closely related to the first kind, that we limit our desires to avoid frustration: If we have an accurate understanding of the way the world is, we also know which desires and aversions are likely to lead to frustration. If we know people are mortal, then we also know that if we want our spouses and children to live forever, we are bound to be disappointed.

Epictetus also cautions us to be aware of the judgments and evaluations we make and to distinguish the judgment we make about a thing from what that thing is itself. We can choose to judge that death is dreadful, or that grades lower than As are disasters; and if we do so, we may be distressed and angry. But these judgments, again, are our own, and if we want to avoid being distressed and angry, it is in our power to change the judgments that make us feel this way [s. 5].

EPICTETUS'S CONCEPTION OF ETHICS

In offering the kind of advice I have described here, Epictetus is responding to what, for the Greeks, was certainly the central question of ethics--"How should one live one's life?" It is not the question one usually finds at the beginning of a modern text on moral philosophy, though the question "how should I live *my* life?" is a question most reflective people ask *themselves* at one time or another.

The answers Epictetus offers are quite specific and detailed. They are the sorts of answers one might find immediately useful and directly applicable to one's situation. There is little in the way of abstract, philosophical theory in the *Handbook*. Indeed, if Epictetus were writing today and had a good publisher, his book would appear between shiny covers, with a picture of soaring gulls on the cover; and it would be found not in the philosophy section of your neighborhood bookstore but under Self-Help. (I say this, I should add, not to denigrate either Epictetus or Self-Help.)

Epictetus's work is an example of the tradition of Greek and Roman ethical thought called the "Stoic" tradition, which flourished for five hundred years. His writings are often included in modern textbooks on ethics as an example of this tradition. In fact, it was in such a textbook that, as an undergraduate, I first encountered the *Handbook*. What now strikes me as most remarkable about this work, however, is how very different it is from the great majority of the books I later learned to think of as the central works in moral philosophy. Part of the reason, as I have already noted, is that there seems to be much advice and very little theory in this work. More relevant to my purposes, though, is the fact that what Epictetus says seems to have little to do with morality, at least as I, and I assume my readers, now think of it.

When I think of morality, of the judgments that are characteristic moral judgments, I think not of advice about what attitudes or beliefs to adopt nor of the suggestion that I might become more aware or perceptive, but of the judgment that something is wrong, or sinful, or the judgment that someone has a right or an obligation. The image that comes to mind is the image of some rule, or law, perhaps like the Ten Commandments, or some method for making decisions like The Golden Rule. And I think of these laws or rules as having an external source of authority, as the criminal law does. If they serve a purpose, it is not the purpose of making *my* life happier but a purpose like protecting the interests of others, promoting the common good, or maybe even the purpose of pleasing a temperamental god.

Epictetus hardly mentions (hardly, but not never--I will come back to this) such rules or laws. He does not talk about moral problems or moral dilemmas in the way we do today. Today, people turn to moral philosophers (or to other specialists in ethics) for help in solving problems, which they see as matters of deciding what is *the right thing to do*. We worry about what morality requires, for example, in medical situations: Is it right to help terminally ill patients die an easy death, or must we do everything we can to prolong life? What about severely handicapped infants or even fetuses? We also worry about whether capital punishment is permissible or whether it is wrong to give priority to minority applicants in college admissions or in hiring decisions.

In all of these cases, and many more, the picture seems to be that there are moral laws or rules, that it is important to comply with them, but that it is not quite clear what they are or what they require. Physicians and patients, pregnant women and fetuses, employers and job applicants, all have, or may have, rights and obligations, but we can't tell what to do until we know just what these rights and obligations are and what they imply.

Epictetus is not motivated by a desire to solve problems like these. At least in the passages I have quoted, what seems to worry him is not the fear that he might do *the wrong thing*. What he offers is not so much judgments, much less commands or prohibitions, but rather pieces of advice. And the advice is intended not to secure compliance with some set of external rules but to help us to live happier, more satisfying lives. If anyone were to ask Epictetus why we should follow his advice, it is pretty obvious how he would reply. He would say that if you do, "your life will go well" [s. 8]. He would say that the things that are "up to us," our attitudes, desires, aversions, and the like, are the "only things that yield freedom and happiness" [s. 1]. By rising above the desires and attitudes we happen to have and rejecting those that don't serve us well, we become the masters of our own lives, and we avoid unnecessary pain and frustration.

HOW GOOD IS EPICTETUS'S ADVICE?

While Epictetus's picture of the nature of ethics is quite different from the modern picture, his conception of how the ethical life, *as he conceives it,* can be justified is a good deal clearer than it is in many modern theories. Implicit in the *Handbook* are answers to a good number of the questions I mentioned in my Introduction. There is an idea of what ethics requires of us, an idea of what its point is, and an idea of what kind of answer we should expect to the question "why be moral?" If Epictetus is right, we will just plain be happier if we do as he suggests. And he may well be right. At least, many people in distress find great consolation in this kind of advice. It seems to improve their lives, or at least make them more content with their lot. Still, it is also possible that Epictetus's advice is not the best. While he intends it to be good advice for someone seeking to live a good live, it may not actually be good advice. There are a number of reasons to think this.

One reason I shall mention now but then put to one side. A lot of what Epictetus recommends seems to have a pretty direct connection with personal well-being, but here and there what he says sounds more like moralistic preaching than like consoling advice:

> Appropriate actions [duties?] are . . . measured by relationships. He is a father: that entails taking care of him, yielding to him in everything, putting up with him when he abuses you or strikes you. "But he is a bad father." Does nature then determine that you have a good father? No, only that you have a father . . . In this way, then, you will discover the appropriate actions to expect from a neighbor, from a citizen, from a general, if you are in the habit of looking at relationships [s. 30].

In addition to moderating our desires, forming realistic expectations, and the like, then, we also apparently are supposed to follow something like rules in our conduct toward others. We are to obey our fathers, be good neighbors and citizens, and [s. 31] obey the gods and even have correct beliefs about them. We should also "set up . . . a certain character and pattern" for ourselves. We should "speak rarely" and only about appropriate subjects; in sexual matters, we should "stay pure as far as possible before marriage"; and, in conversation, we should "stay away from making frequent and long-winded mention of what you have done" [s. 33].

Now, there is some question, in my mind, whether strict obedience to a father or to the gods is the kind of thing that tends to make one happy. Epictetus would insist that the policy of obedience is one that we ought to choose, freely, for ourselves, so that, in a sense, we remain our own masters. And by limiting our other desires--by learning to take abuse with equanimity, for example--we can mitigate the costs of acquiescing in the authority of others. But then everything hinges on whether the advice that one should learn to minimize desires and to want only what is in one's power is good advice. That is the question to which I now want to turn.

People who are aware of the world around them, who have accurate, realistic expectations, and who have learned to desire, or care about, only the things they can be certain of attaining, are likely to be, almost by definition, *contented.* They will not suffer frustration, disappointment, or regret. They won't be angry or resentful. They will accept their lot with tranquility. But will they be happy? Can we reasonably say that they live good lives? Well, someone might say that such people must be happy, simply on the ground that whatever desires they have are satisfied. But we should be aware of what this answer assumes. It assumes that the only issue in choosing desires is whether they are freely chosen and whether they are or are not easily satisfied. If that were true, then we would maximize our chances of being happy simply by freely and consciously choosing desires that were the easiest ones to satisfy. But it may not be true. It may be that there is more satisfaction, sometimes, in goals that are more uncertain and difficult to reach.

Most of us, in the course of our lives, develop new interests, even passions, and many of us feel that our lives are greatly enriched by them. We discard old interests, and we find new ones, new hobbies, new sports, new friends, new careers, or new aspects of careers we already have. These new interests often challenge us, leading us to discover talents we didn't know we had, and they absorb our interest. We feel that our lives are better, not simply because more of our old desires are satisfied but because we have found new sources of satisfaction and because the new satisfactions are sometimes deeper. But the deeper satisfactions may not be as easy to achieve as the older, less deep ones.

The experiences I describe here are, I hope, familiar to my readers. If I am right, it is important to be aware of them. These possibilities have a great deal to do, for example, with how we raise and educate our children: If we care about their well-being, we need to provide them with the opportunity to experience a variety of possible interests and the capacity to develop new interests and the skills these interests demand. But now I am getting ahead of myself. The question I have been raising is whether we can assume people are living well if all we know about them is that their desires are satisfied and they do not suffer disappointment. What I have claimed is that people whose desires are satisfied might not be as well off as they could be--if they had acquired and satisfied more profound desires and interests. Perhaps the point could be put this way: One dimension of well-being is contentment, the degree to which we avoid frustration and disappointment; but a second dimension has to do with the *richness* of our lives, the variety and depth of the satisfactions life affords us.[2] Offhand, there is likely to be a trade-off between these two. The kind of life, the attitude toward life, that offers the richest possibilities may also open the door to frustration and dissatisfaction. One need only think of the commitment to raise a family or to enter a competitive profession.

What I say here may, of course, be mistaken. I certainly don't think I have proved it. I can only ask my readers to reflect on their own experience. But whether or not what I say about happiness or well-being is right, what I think I have shown is that what Epictetus says rests on certain assumptions that are not *obviously* true.

So far, I have spoken as if Epictetus's key assumption is an assumption about the nature of happiness: A contented life, freely chosen and devoid of frustration, is a happy one. But there are other possible ways to interpret him. Perhaps, for example, he is just a pessimist. He may agree with me that, if we are lucky, we can live far happier lives than the life of mere contentment--*but* the world is such a harsh place and other people are so unpredictable and unreasonable that we are almost certain to be disappointed if we set our sights high. It is true, after all, that Epictetus was a slave much of his life and that he lived in Rome during a period of great turmoil--during the time when Nero was emperor and not long after the reigns of Tiberius and Caligula. And perhaps in circumstances like these, Epictetus's attitude is the best one to take. Indeed, in many of our lives, there are times when it is best to set our sights lower and to learn to find satisfaction where we can. But this falls short of recommending Epictetus's attitude as a good general guide to life.

Another possibility, slightly different, is that he is not pessimistic but is, as modern decision theorists would put it, "risk averse." Someone who is risk averse, roughly, is someone who worries far more about the possibility of loss than about any possible gain. An extreme form of risk aversion leads to what is called a "maximin" attitude toward planning: Choose a plan by looking only at the worst possible outcome of each plan and then select the one with the least-bad worst outcome (i.e., choose the plan with the *max*imum *min*imum payoff). This is, to say the least, a very conservative attitude. It is the attitude of a football coach who would never call a pass play because, after all, the pass *might* be intercepted. But someone with such an attitude might advocate the kind of life Epictetus advocates even if he or she admitted that there were possible greater advantages to other lives. It is just that the possible losses are also greater and, to a risk averse chooser, that settles it.

A final possibility is that Epictetus, or someone like him, could think that the attitudes he recommends are a *good strategy* for dealing with life, and perhaps especially for dealing with other people, in the sense that minimizing desires or learning to control desires *indirectly* makes it easier to attain the various goals one does have. People who are too demanding, too "needy," as it is sometimes put, drive others away. Perhaps, paradoxically, if we want less, we get more.

Now, to repeat, it is not my aim to try to defend one of these interpretations as the only correct one. What each represents is a possible way of defending the main kinds of advice Epictetus offers. People who accept this advice may do it for any of these reasons or, indeed, for some further reason. If they want to defend it (to themselves or to someone else) they need to give some reason, and they need to be prepared to defend the reason, too! (Is it really true that we will get more from life if we seek less? Perhaps.)

CONCLUSION: THE LIMITS OF THE STOIC PERSPECTIVE

As philosophical works go, the *Handbook* of Epictetus is relatively straightforward. It is not difficult to understand, at least in a general way, what kinds of behavior and attitude Epictetus means to recommend, nor is it difficult to understand what he takes to be the *point* of his recommendations. Moreover, since it is quite clear how Epictetus understands the purpose of his inquiry, it is also easy to see what kind of arguments or evidence we need either to support or criticize his theory. To a large extent, his conclusions amount to practical advice, based on experience of life. Just as an experienced carpenter can teach techniques to an apprentice, so also, Epictetus seems to think, can someone with experience of life in general teach others how to live better. And surely there is something to this analogy. After all, people do go to parents, friends, and sometimes psychotherapists just because these other people have experience dealing with life's problems and sometimes know what to do. Of course, the aims of life in general are less concrete and more controversial than the aims of a craft like carpentry. Even people who agree that they want to be happy may disagree about what happiness is. Indeed, one of my main criticisms has been that Epictetus may have a limited or eccentric conception of happiness. Yet even here, it is quite possible that experience with life can at least help us come to a better understanding of this idea and even to some level of agreement. Whether that is so remains to be seen.

If we think of the ethical life in the way Epictetus does, it is relatively easy to make a good, prima facie case that people who want to be happy have a reason to lead such a life. We can give one of the possible kinds of answer to the question "why be moral?" But it is important to see that we can give this answer only because of the particular way in which Epictetus approaches ethics, only because of the particular conception of the ethical life that he offers. This echoes a general point I made in my Introduction: We cannot answer the question "why be moral?" unless we also offer some account of what being moral is like; and whether we can plausibly offer answers of a certain kind--in this case, an answer in terms of personal happiness--depends on how we conceive the requirements of morality. Epictetus makes it easy because, after all, he pretty clearly thinks of ethics in general as the study of how one should live in order to live a happy life. That is "what's in it for me."

From our point of view, there are at least two reasons why the *Handbook* might seem inadequate as a response to the questions that initially led us to the study of ethics. First, many of us are likely to approach ethics with *moral problems* in mind--problems about the permissibility of things like euthanasia, abortion, or affirmative action. We want to be told what is the right thing to do in these matters, and Epictetus seems not even to ask questions like this. (Most of us, I assume, will not be satisfied with answers like "accept whatever happens," "don't try to change the world," or, even "do whatever you want, and just accept that it doesn't really matter.")

On reflection, it is perhaps not surprising that Epictetus does not attempt to answer questions like these. What he focuses on is what a person needs to live a happy life; but the moral problems I have described, especially problems like affirmative action (and *maybe* abortion), involve *conflicts* of interest between persons. What is good for one may not be good for the other. Any solution to the problem may be bad for someone. The question is not what one or the other needs to live well, but, rather, whether there is any way to reconcile the good of one with the good of the other--even, in the worst cases, which one lives well and which doesn't. This kind of question must be answered from a standpoint separate from that of any particular party to a dispute. It is tempting to say that it needs to be answered from a *moral* standpoint, except that, so far, we have no definition of what that means. In any case, if we take a point of view different from either particular party's, it seems likely that it will be hard to show that both individuals have a reason to go along with our decision. It may require that one or both end up with less than is wanted.

Epictetus's approach to ethics, then, is limited; but that is not the point on which I have mainly concentrated. I have focused more on the second reason we might find what Epictetus says inadequate, namely, that his advice seems to presuppose a controversial conception of human well-being. Though it is easy to see *some* connection between what he advises us to do and *some* of the elements of happiness as we understand it, there is still good reason to doubt that his advice is anything like the best advice. Thus, even if we think the basic question of ethics is the question how one should live to achieve happiness or well-being, the answer depends on the answer to a prior question-- "what is the good or happy life?" By the time Epictetus wrote, it seems, a consensus had formed among the Stoics on the answer: A good life is a contented, tranquil life, free from frustration or pain. A few hundred years earlier, however, when Aristotle was writing, there was no such consensus. "What is the good life?" is the question with which Aristotle begins; and as we shall see, he gives a very different answer from the one Epictetus assumes.

2

HAPPINESS AND THE VIRTUES

ARISTOTLE, 384-322 B.C.

Aristotle was born in Stagira, in what is now northern Greece, some four centuries before Epictetus. Greek philosophy was at its height. Aristotle came to Athens, where he studied with Plato, who, in turn, had been a student and follower of Socrates. Aristotle's works cover many subjects, and they include more than one book just on ethics. I will discuss only the *Nicomachean Ethics*.[1] Like all of Aristotle's extant works, this is probably something like a compilation of Aristotle's lecture notes. It may be called "Nicomachean" because it was edited or compiled by a pupil named Nicomachus.

At the beginning of his *Nicomachean Ethics*, Aristotle says, "Every craft and every investigation, and likewise every action and decision, seems to aim at some good; hence the good has been well described as that at which everything aims" [1094a, 1-4]. The point of the *Ethics* is to explain what the good is, for "knowledge of this good is . . . of great importance for the conduct of our lives, and, if, like archers, we have a target to aim at, we are more likely to hit the right mark" [1094a, 24-27].

I interpret the first passage quoted to mean, simply, that whenever we act, we do so for some purpose. When Aristotle speaks of a "good," he has in mind a purpose which someone has, or, perhaps better, should have. He then notes that though different acts have different immediate goals, those goals themselves are usually sought for the sake of some further goal, and he conjectures, without fully committing himself on this point, that for each of us, there is only one final or ultimate goal: Whatever a person does is done, ultimately, for the sake of that goal, and a person's good is to be identified with that goal. Once people become clear about what their own basic goals are, they will be able to plan and organize their lives more effectively.

Aristotle concludes rather quickly [Bk. i, Ch. 4] that the ultimate aim, the good, for each of us, is happiness, or well-being. But he finds the claim that each of us seeks happiness to be unhelpful. To say that we seek happiness tells us no more than that we seek what is good for us. It does not give us any additional help in planning or organizing our lives. Hence, the basic question of the book remains--"what is the good (for each), or, equivalently, what does happiness consist in?"

Before going on, we need to note two things. First, it may seem obvious to most of us that the good or happy life for me, say, is likely to be different from the good or happy life for someone else. We have different tastes, needs, and abilities. (I have very little musical ability, for example, so a musical life, for me, would be just embarrassing and frustrating. For other people, it can be wonderful.) So, we might wonder how Aristotle could hope to answer, in a general way, a question like "what is good for a person?" But Aristotle does not assume that, in every detail, a good life for me will be like a good life for you. He need only assume that it is possible to say something general but informative about what (otherwise different) good lives have in common. Perhaps, for example, the good life for anyone involves developing and exercising his or her particular talents. For you, that may mean a musical career; for me, perhaps, an academic one.

Second, in the first passage I quoted, Aristotle seems to describe the good as what everyone *does* aim at, and he seems to suggest, therefore, that we can find out, for each of us, what the good or happy life is simply by careful examination of what it is we actually seek. It quickly becomes clear, however, that that is not Aristotle's assumption. In Book i, Chapter 5, he describes various basic goals people actually have--pleasure, honor, money-making, virtue--and, while not denying that people do have these goals, he argues that they are not reasonable. They are not goals we *should* pursue if we want to live well and be happy. So, Aristotle's idea is not that the good is whatever one does aim at, but, rather, what one would aim at if one were choosing rationally.

What Aristotle concludes, in rough summary, is that one needs to develop certain "excellences" (or "virtues" as it is normally translated) and that one should seek to live an active life, exercising these excellences. The excellences a person should develop and exercise include various talents and skills that Aristotle refers to as virtues of thought, and they also include a number of virtues of character, many of which (e.g., justice, courage, and temperance) we would today call moral virtues. A large part of the *Nicomachean Ethics* consists of an analysis of these virtues and other forms of excellence, though there are also discussions of such topics as friendship and pleasure. What

Aristotle seems to think is that, if one develops and exercises the human excellences, and if one also has reasonably good fortune in health and the other external circumstances of one's life, one will live happily [Bk. i, Chs. 7-12].

What we can see here, I think, are a number of similarities between Aristotle's approach to ethics and that of Epictetus; but we can also see differences. Both want to offer an account of how one should live one's life, and both assume that the account should be an account of how to live in order to live well or be happy. That, as I have said before, was the issue of ethics as the Greeks saw it. Aristotle, though, goes a good deal further than Epictetus does. While each gives a relatively specific account of just how one should live or what one should do, Aristotle also tries to locate this account in a more general theory of the nature of well-being itself. While Epictetus seemed to make some assumptions about the nature of happiness, Aristotle actually addresses the question of what it is and so is able to give, at least in outline, an explanation of *why* one needs to live as he recommends. And his definition of happiness differs from the one Epictetus seems to assume. Moreover, while the advice Epictetus offered included little of what *we* might ordinarily think of as moral advice, Aristotle tries to analyze and defend various moral virtues. He tries to show that these virtues can be justified by showing that they contribute to the well-being of those who have them. Whether he is successful in showing this is one of my main questions. To answer it, we need to examine his argument.

ARISTOTLE'S ARGUMENT

If Aristotle is right, when we begin with the question of what kind of life is a happy life, we will find out that one does well to develop the aims and attitudes that make up the moral virtues. And the moral virtues that he has in mind do not amount just to limiting desires, having true beliefs about the world, and avoiding commitments as Epictetus said we should. For Aristotle, the virtues have a much more active aspect. As Aristotle conceives the ethical life, it involves dispositions, tendencies to act and choose, of the kind most of us would regard as moral dispositions. These include the disposition to be truthful, to be generous, and to be temperate (i.e., to have the appropriate appetites, neither too much nor too little, for sensual pleasures). This conclusion clearly depends on Aristotle's basic ideas about the nature of happiness. Why should we accept these ideas, and just exactly what is the connection between well-being and the virtues?

Aristotle begins, I have said, with the question of what is the good for a person. When we know the answer, we will know what to aim at; and Aristotle seems to assume that leading a good or happy life is a matter of effectively pursuing the right aims or goals. Some people go wrong by having the wrong aims, and one thing Aristotle does in Book i of the *Ethics* is to propose and defend some general criteria for choosing aims.

In Book i, Chapter 5, as previously mentioned, Aristotle surveys some of the goals people actually have: pleasure, honor, virtue, the life of study, and money-making, for example; and he offers interesting reasons for rejecting some of these. Thus, for example, he says that the pursuit of honor (something like political popularity) is not reasonable because its attainment depends too much on what others happen to think, and others can be fickle. Again, the single-minded pursuit of money is a mistake, for money is merely useful, not intrinsically satisfying. Nor, interestingly, does he think the attainment of virtue a reasonable conception of the good, for the possession of virtue, by itself, is inadequate to make a life good or happy. It is "too incomplete." A person might be virtuous but still suffer "the worst evils and misfortunes" [1096a, 1].

Each of these reasons for rejecting some particular conception of the good tells us something about what kind of goal Aristotle thinks we *should* adopt. First, we should be sure to organize our lives around the pursuit of things that are *ends*, not mere means--we should aim at something satisfying in itself. (That is why money-making is not reasonable as an ultimate goal.) Second, we should aim at something, unlike honor, which is within our own power to attain and to keep. Third, we should not settle for a goal or goals that are incomplete. Aristotle stresses this idea, mentioning it again a few pages later, in Chapter 7, where he speaks of the good as something "self-sufficient." What we should aim at is there described as something that "all by itself . . . makes a life choiceworthy and lacking in nothing." Happiness, he says, is complete, or self-sufficient, in this sense, "since it is not counted as one good among many." Nothing could be added to it that would make it any better [1097b, 8-21].

I suggest that this idea of completeness, or self-sufficiency, is actually two different ideas compressed into one. The more obvious idea, what I call quantitative completeness, is that one should include in one's plans as many different intrinsically satisfying goals as possible. Why settle for less if more is possible? The second idea, which I call qualitative completeness, is that if two competing goals differ in that one is in itself more fully satisfying, one should prefer the more satisfying one.

The idea that one's life can be better and happier if one has more of the things one finds satisfying, or if the things that one does are more satisfying in themselves, is an important idea. It seems to fit with my experience, at least. But it is an idea that plays no role in Epictetus's thinking about how to live. His idea is not to find out what kinds of activity are most completely satisfying in themselves, but rather to find out how to avoid certain kinds of frustration or disappointment. While Epictetus focuses on how to avoid being discontented, Aristotle seeks to find how much better one can do over and above being merely contented.

It is true, of course, that Aristotle is not unaware of the dangers of disappointment. He advocates not only that one seek the most completely satisfying goals but also that one avoid aims the achievement of which are not in one's own control. This was the objection to making honor one's ultimate aim and, on that point, Aristotle sounded a lot like Epictetus. But this creates a potential problem within Aristotle's theory. There is clearly a possibility that the best goals, from the point of view of qualitative and quantitative completeness, will not be the wisest according to the requirement that they be within one's own power. We may have to make a trade-off between security and full satisfaction. Still, it seems to me to be an advantage of Aristotle's theory that he at least recognizes the problem. And, as it happens, he *thinks* that there is a kind of life that is both within our power and fully satisfying. This kind of life, he says in Chapter 7, is a life that involves "the soul's activity that expresses virtue" [1098a, 17]. What does this mean, and how does Aristotle come to this conclusion?

What is striking about Aristotle's procedure, I think, is that after developing the general criteria I have described, he does not apply them directly to the defense of his own theory. Instead, in the middle of Chapter 7, he abruptly raises the question of what the "function," or distinctive capacity, of a human being is and then quickly concludes that since our distinctive capacity is rational activity (the activity of the soul), the good life is the life of virtuous (or excellent) activities involving the use of reason. Rational activity is the distinctive activity of our species, but why is the right question a question about function, or distinctive ability? Why think that doing what is distinctively human is doing what is most satisfying? Why think it is satisfying at all? And, finally, why must the activities be activities that "express virtue?"

Aristotle does not answer these questions explicitly, but it is possible to imagine answers that he might have offered and that also have some plausibility. He might have reasoned, first, that what creatures do naturally tends to be satisfying. Aristotle did not himself have an evolutionary theory of biology, but he did study animals and was aware that they were often well adapted to their environments. Now, if the natural capacities they have are the ones they need to use, and if they will use them only if doing so tends to be satisfying, then, if they are well adapted, the exercise of their natural capacities will tend to be satisfying. Anyhow, regardless of whether Aristotle would have given an argument like this, experience provides some informal evidence for the conclusion that activities involving capacities for planning, calculating, strategic reasoning, and the like tend to be enjoyable. People like games and puzzles, and they find those that are relatively difficult but not impossible even more enjoyable. This last point, namely, that they are not impossible, needs to be emphasized. People like complex and difficult activities, *when they can do them at some reasonable level of proficiency* but not when they are frustrating. (We don't like math problems when we can't even figure out how to start; we hate golf until we begin to hit some good shots.)

If we are willing to make these assumptions, then it is possible to understand how Aristotle, starting with the general criteria he lays out early in Book i, could come to the particular conception of the good life he settles on in Chapter 7. Moreover, these assumptions make that conception plausible. By developing and exercising one's natural capacities for activities involving the use of reason, and by doing them well (in a way that "expresses virtue"), one contributes to one's happiness. Moreover, not only is the skillful exercise of developed capacities intrinsically satisfying, but it is also something that is largely under one's own control. Unlike the life of money-making, or the pursuit of honor, success in this kind of activity is not overly subject to fickle fate and the whims of others.

Aristotle himself, I should emphasize again, does not work out the reasoning for his conclusion in the way I have. It is interesting, though, that, in the course of a discussion of pleasure in Book x, he says some things about pleasant activities that fit nicely with this account of the good. The activities that we consider pleasant, he says there, are just the activities that we tend to do intensely. The intensity of our activity is a mark of its pleasantness. Pleasure increases concentration, and that, in turn, increases the activity. The skill with which one engages in the activity and the quality of one's awareness of what one sees or experiences make the pleasure greater. Conversely, when other enjoyments, "alien pleasures," interfere with concentration, pleasure in the first activity diminishes [Bk. x, Ch. 4]. In general, then, pleasure or enjoyment involves something like concentration, being absorbed in something.[2] Enjoyment might best be understood as the absence of boredom. And as I noted above, for many of us, the activities that hold our attention, that are not boring, are those that involve our rational abilities and at which we have some skill.

SOME QUALIFICATIONS

If these ideas are plausible, then there is some reason to agree with Aristotle that rational activities are a major element in many happy lives. There is also some reason to think that these lives, at least, depend for their quality partly on one's having acquired certain virtues, or excellences, namely, certain skills at strategy, planning, calculating, and understanding. A number of qualifications, however, are in order.

First, though Aristotle himself sometimes (especially in the second half of Book x) expresses a preference for a life of study or contemplation, nothing in his explicit argument or in the supplementary argument I have provided supports such a narrow, intellectualist interpretation of the idea of rational activity in his account of the good life. The intrinsic satisfactions of intellectual activity are present as much in managing a baseball team as in doing mathematics or philosophy. Indeed, though one might be tempted to infer from Aristotle's emphasis on intellectual activity that only an intelligent elite could live really good and happy lives, a more reasonable inference from the argument I have presented is that each person does best to develop his or her particular rational capacities and talents and to exercise them in activities that are relatively challenging and absorbing. This way of putting the point, of course, allows that there may be a considerable variety of good kinds of life, and also that, for virtually anyone, there is some kind of life that is good. Nevertheless, it is still consistent with Aristotle's basic idea that any good life requires the development and exercise of excellences.

Second, one of Aristotle's criteria for evaluating possible conceptions of the kind of life to lead was completeness, or self-sufficiency: A conception of what to aim at is unreasonable if it leaves out interests, needs, or sources of satisfaction that could be included and that would make life even better. And, by this standard, no matter how absorbing "rational activities" might be, they hardly make for a fully happy life. They are merely "one good among many," and Aristotle sometimes recognizes this. After offering his definition of the good in Book i, Chapter 7, he makes a number of qualifications and additions in the next five chapters, and he notes especially that happiness requires adequate "external" goods and "goods of fortune"--health, friends, family, and adequate material circumstances. And so he concludes, "The happy person is the one who expresses complete virtue in his activities, with an adequate supply of external goods, not for just any time but for a complete life" [1101a, 15f].

Finally, while a convincing argument can be constructed to show that the development of certain virtues, or excellences, namely, certain rational skills, contributes directly to one's well-being, there is nothing in the argument so far to show that the *moral* virtues contribute to happiness. Yet Aristotle, in the last chapter of Book i, writes as if this has already been shown. Taking it for granted that the moral virtues promote one's own well-being, he then proceeds, in Books ii-v, to discuss them in some detail. What are these virtues, and why should we think they promote one's happiness?

MORAL VIRTUES AND THE GOOD

Aristotle discusses a number of virtues, including bravery, temperance, truthfulness, wittiness, generosity, and justice. Conspicuously lacking are some of the cardinal Christian virtues of faith, hope, and charity (understood to require a more extensive general benevolence than Aristotle's generosity). Aristotle offers no general reason for picking just these virtues, and it is noteworthy not only that certain virtues that might appear on modern lists are missing but also that he includes things *we* might not regard as moral matters at all--wittiness, for example, and also a notion of magnanimity that has something to do with expecting to be honored appropriately by others. That his list of moral virtues differs some from modern lists is interesting, but I wish to focus my attention on the idea that the virtues he does mention, and which we are likely to regard as moral virtues, are good for their possessor. How could Aristotle argue for this?

Aristotle emphasizes that the moral virtues, as well as the intellectual virtues, all involve the exercise of the distinctive human capacity for reason. Virtues like bravery, temperance, and justice require ability at planning and calculating. However, from the fact that the exercise of reason in "intellectual" activities is intrinsically satisfying, it does not follow that it is satisfying in all its employments. While there is often some intrinsic satisfaction in the exercise of the "virtues" (skills) of a mathematician, I have always found it implausible that there is much intrinsic satisfaction in the exercise of the moral virtues. (Proving a theorem can be exciting and even fun. Being brave may be necessary to some end, but it is not something one usually finds intrinsically satisfying.) In my opinion, therefore, if there is reason to think we are better off having the moral virtues than not, it is most likely that the reason has to do with their effects. This may not be Aristotle's own view; but it is worth noting that, for some of the virtues, including bravery, temperance, and wit, it is not hard to make the case that they do have good effects for their possessors. We do not need bravery, for example, only in battle or only when called upon to rescue a stranger from a burning house. We need to be brave to ask for a raise, to take a difficult course in college, or to stand up for our rights in a hostile environment. Temperance, understood as involving moderation in appetites for sensual pleasures like food, drink, and sex, can obviously help us avoid the bad consequences of overindulgence. (Consider the hangover.) And being witty, of course, makes it easier to get dates.

Now, in suggesting that Aristotle might make these arguments (he does not make them explicitly), I am making use of the fact that he does not define the happy life *merely* as the life of pure intellectual activity. I am assuming that he regards friendship, health, and decent material circumstances as parts of the good life. But, even if one concedes that some of Aristotle's virtues can contribute to happiness, what I have said falls far short of showing that being moral is really desirable as a means to happiness. There are at least two points here. First, many people who deny that morality is good for us would still agree that things like wit and moderation in desires are useful. It is just that those are not *moral* virtues as we now understand them. (They are no more matters of morality than were the various attitudes and habits of mind Epictetus advocated.)

Second, while at least some of the virtues I have mentioned can sometimes do us some good (by preventing hangovers, for example) they may, on the whole, do us more harm. Bravery and temperance can have good consequences but also bad ones. Bravery does expose us to risks, and temperance does limit our sources of pleasure. Death and serious injury are not goods, and a life that is cramped and joyless, even if it is long and healthy, is not all that great.

It is possible to respond to these points in a way that is consistent at least with the spirit of Aristotle's work. To begin with, Aristotle himself does include among the virtues not only traits like temperance and wit but also more standardly "moral" traits like generosity, truthfulness, and justice; but it is possible to argue that these, too, can contribute to one's well-being. It must be admitted, of course, that particular acts of generosity or justice are not without cost. When we give gifts or donate to charity, and when we refrain from taking more than our share or when we yield to the rights of others, there is often some immediate sacrifice involved. But to defend the claim that the *virtues* of justice or generosity are good for us, Aristotle need not insist that *particular acts* manifesting these virtues are always costless. All he need show is that we are better off, overall, having these traits than not having them. And there are, surely, some benefits. People are grateful for acts of kindness and generosity, and they resent injustice. They won't cooperate with people who won't reciprocate, and they won't trust habitual liars. Hence, if we make the assumption that people benefit from having friends and that they sometimes need the willing cooperation of others, and if we also assume that others will not befriend those who are selfish and will not cooperate with those who are unfair, it looks as if people concerned with their own well-being have a reason to have the virtues of justice and generosity.

The argument has now become quite elaborate, and it will become more elaborate yet. Notice several crucial assumptions that have already been made. First, it is important that Aristotle seems willing to include, in his conception of the happy life, such things as friends, family, and the material benefits of social cooperation. If these were not things that tend to make a life better, then the argument that we benefit from virtues like generosity and justice would not work. Second, I am certainly assuming a society in which there is a good deal of agreement about, for example, what justice requires, and I am also assuming that people are perceptive enough to know, for example, when they are being cheated and by whom. Finally, I should reiterate that the argument is an argument that one will benefit from having certain *virtues*, not that, for example, every act of justice yields a net benefit. This last point deserves more comment.

Someone might suggest that, even given the assumptions I have made, the best strategy for a person seeking to live a happy life would be to act generously and justly, *sometimes*--just enough to get a good reputation, and just when it doesn't cost too much. The ideal attitude, this person would say, is the attitude of a clever calculator who cultivates the appearance of being trustworthy and cooperative, but who does whatever is best for himself when he can get away with it. Now, such a person would not have the virtues of justice or generosity, according to Aristotle's definition of virtue.[3] To have these virtues, a person must actually *want* to share and not to take what belongs to another. It is a sign of having a virtue, Aristotle says, that one takes pleasure in doing virtuous acts and does them for their own sake [1104b, 5f; 1105a, 30f]. One may have other desires that conflict with these, of course, but to the extent that one has the virtues, the virtuous desires will simply be stronger. So the question is whether, given that it is in one's interest to appear to have the virtues and so to act virtuously in some cases, it is better actually to have the virtues or to pursue a clever strategy of the kind described above.

There are a couple of relevant considerations here. First, the most direct way to *appear* to have the virtues, obviously, is just to *have* them. And this may be the easiest way, too. The virtuous life, as Aristotle pictures it, is not a life of struggle. In modern jargon, the virtues are fully "internalized." Virtuous people who act virtuously are actually doing what they want to do. They do what, to them, comes naturally. The life of strategic calculation, by contrast, seems to be a life of conflict and struggle. One often does what morality demands, but only under a kind of duress, only as a means to an end. And when one can get away with it, one acts otherwise--but with stealth. And that itself is costly. It is not always easy to hide and conceal. (*Conscientious* self-interest may be as hard as a conscientious commitment to moral duty. Indeed, it involves something like making a duty out of self-interest.) If all this is right, then there is much to be said for the virtues.

This argument proceeds, it should be noted, by means of a comparison of costs and benefits, and one crucial question is just how much one sacrifices when one has the moral virtues, just how much one would gain if one didn't. (Virtuous people, recall, don't really *think* about cheating, even when the opportunity presents itself. How much do they forego?) This question also concerns the issue I raised earlier when I wondered about the virtue of temperance--whether, though it obviously has some advantages, these advantages were worth the cost. Does temperance involve total disregard of sensual pleasure? Do justice, truthfulness, or generosity require great sacrifice in terms of other goods? This brings us to the second consideration in favor of Aristotle's virtues.

Aristotle's tendency is to give a definition of the virtues according to which they do not require too much. Thus, in general, he thinks of the virtues as requiring acts that fall in a kind of *mean* between extremes: Brave people are not cowardly, but neither do they foolishly disregard their personal safety; temperate people do not overindulge, but neither do they totally avoid the pleasures of food, drink, and sex; and just people do not take more than their share, but they are not required to take any less. So, it seems, Aristotle would probably deny that the virtues are too burdensome. However, this talk of virtue as a means is all very imprecise. Aristotle simply does not tell us much about just how to calculate it; and in important cases, like the case of justice (to which he devotes the whole of Book v), his account remains rather schematic. It requires, for example, respect for the law in one's relations with others, but he does not say what the law should require.

(What if the law is oppressive, one wonders?) It requires that we not take more than our share and that we distribute common funds justly, but he does not say just how we determine fair shares.

CONCLUSION: ARISTOTLE'S ACHIEVEMENTS AND THEIR LIMITS

Clearly, Aristotle leaves a lot of questions unanswered. It is possible to draw only conditional conclusions about his theory: Given his account of the nature of the good life, it is clear that a person derives significant benefits from having virtues like bravery, temperance, and wit. Moreover, if we specify the requirements of virtues like justice in such a way that they are not too burdensome for those who have them, while still advancing the good of others, and if there is general agreement that these requirements *are* the requirements, then it will promote one's good, as Aristotle understands the good, to have this virtue. People who are seen by others as being just and truthful will be able to secure the trust and cooperation of others when they need it; and there is no doubt that we sometimes need trust and cooperation. Still, even these conditional conclusions require some further qualification.

First, the kind of life Aristotle describes as a good life--a rich, full and active life, lived among friends with similar or complementary interests and involving the active exercise of developed rational capacities--is, I am prepared to believe, a happy life. As Aristotle would agree, this is certainly enough for a good life; great relative wealth or competitive success of the kind that involves doing better than others is not necessary. Nothing in the argument so far shows, however, that Aristotle's is the *only* kind of happy life; and, in very unfortunate circumstances (e.g., if one were a slave, like Epictetus, or if one lived in conditions of grave scarcity or a disintegrating social structure), aiming at such a life might only produce frustration and disappointment. Second, while we can conclude, conditionally, that the virtues tend to promote personal well-being, it has not been shown that they are *necessary* for happiness--certainly not that any person must have all of them to be happy. Experience suggests that people who are, say, brave, temperate, and witty, but less than fully just, can do very well for themselves. But none of this means that we can do very well with *none* of the virtues, and neither does it mean that having the virtues is not generally a benefit. It is certainly possible, subject to the conditions outlined above, to live a fully virtuous life that is also a very good life indeed. Being moral, in the sense of possessing the

Aristotelian virtues, is not some kind of personal disaster. Even if the kind of life that essentially involves these virtues is not the only kind of life that is good, it is by no means clear that any other kind of life is better.

I am inclined, indeed, to go further than this. In raising children, one can hardly do better than to help them develop attitudes and dispositions of the kind I have discussed--truthfulness, generosity, a sense of justice, moderation in appetites, and a good sense of humor. One does well by one's children, and by others, in raising them this way. As Aristotle sees this, though, it is much more a matter of acquiring certain aims and habits of mind than of learning rigid rules; and it is not a matter of becoming self-denying. Aristotle's virtues, by and large, do not require that we give up our natural aims and desires, but just that we pursue them only in ways consistent with, for example, the demands of honesty and justice. No doubt, we teach this best by example. But here I am going beyond anything for which I have seriously argued.

Before leaving Aristotle, it is important to take note of some of the limitations of his theory. Consider, again, the virtue of justice. This seems to require, as Aristotle sees it, that we give people what they deserve, that we share common resources fairly, that we not cheat one another in transactions, and that we refrain from theft and similar violations of rights. And I have pointed out that, when there is general agreement on what people deserve, what shares are fair, and what belongs to whom, it is likely to be in one's interest to be just. But suppose we now think about the kind of moral issue that people confront in today's society. A person who is committed to justice, a just person, is likely to be faced with difficult choices in situations in which there are sharp disagreements about what the right thing to do is and no general agreement even on how to resolve the disagreement. One need only reflect for a minute on issues like abortion, capital punishment, euthanasia, affirmative action, or redistributive taxation to realize that people are deeply divided about just what rights and obligations we have.

Aristotle thinks, of course, that people ought to respect rights, that justice requires it, but he offers no general way to decide what rights people have. He offers no general way to determine the *content* of the virtue of justice. More important, he cannot do so within the kind of theory he seeks to develop. The basic question for Aristotle, as for Epictetus, is the question "what is best for an individual?" Given a general answer to this question, one can then propose more specific ideas about how a particular person should live in order to live as good a life as possible. But questions about what rights people have, like the question of whether women ever have a right to choose abortion or whether affirmative action is ever legitimate, are questions about what to do when there is a conflict between the interests of different persons (or, in some cases, between persons and the possible interests of potential future persons). Knowing what would be best for each hardly tells us who should prevail when they cannot both have what would be best. Granted, in a later work, the *Politics*, Aristotle does discuss social arrangements, and he is aware that different kinds of arrangements will have different consequences for who lives well. My point, though, is that the theory of the good life in the *Ethics* does not provide him with a way of answering the question of which arrangements we should prefer.

One idea is that the point of rights or rules of justice and fairness is to provide a fair guide for resolving conflicts of interest. When we know what rights people have, we know who gets to make which decisions and who gets to have which goods--and, if the rights are as they should be, the division of goods and authority is a fair one. But which systems of rights are fair? That question can be answered, it would seem, not from the perspective of a concern with any one person's good but only from a point of view that is in some way impartial among persons--one that somehow takes into account and strikes a balance among the claims of all.

The major philosophers of the modern period (the seventeenth century to the present) have concentrated less on questions about the nature of individual well-being and much more on the kind of question I have just described--questions about what rights and obligations people have with respect to one another. Indeed, for these philosophers, that is what ethics or morality is mainly about. And modern philosophers propose and defend answers to these questions by trying to show that their answers are best when considered from some standpoint that reflects the interests of people generally, not just from the standpoint of some one individual. However, just as Epictetus and Aristotle differ about how, in detail, one should live one's life, modern philosophers also differ about what rights and obligations people have. Moreover, just as Aristotle and Epictetus seem to disagree about how to live because they disagree about what the good life is, so also do modern philosophers disagree on specific questions at least partly because there is more than one standpoint that can be said to be impartial among persons, more than one way to take into account the interests of everyone. Thus, for example, some have emphasized the idea of trying to promote total happiness or well-being, and others have focused on trying to find systems of rights and obligations that are acceptable to each person. Much of modern moral philosophy has revolved around the question of which of these standpoints is the right standpoint from which to view moral questions. The next four chapters, in one way or another, will all be concerned with this issue.

One final nod to Aristotle, however, is not inappropriate. What we have seen is that given certain assumptions about the good life, it may be true that it is in one's interest to have moral virtues, like the virtue of justice. People may live happier lives if they take a genuine interest in being fair and respecting the rights of others. But, we have also seen that whether this is plausible depends, in part, on what the virtues require, on what, in particular, justice demands. I have also said, however, that the question of what rights people have, and so what the virtue of justice actually requires, needs to be answered from a standpoint different from that of any particular individual. As we develop an account of the requirements of morality as conceived from this more general standpoint, we will have to reconsider the question of what reason people could have, if any, to comply with these requirements. A more specific question, from the perspective of Aristotelian philosophy, is whether virtues like justice, defined from a suitably impartial perspective, will still be beneficial to particular persons concerned with advancing their own good. I will return to these questions repeatedly in the following chapters.

PART TWO

Modern
Moral Philosophy

3

THE MORAL POINT OF VIEW

IMMANUEL KANT, 1724-1804

Immanuel Kant was born and lived his whole life in Koenigsberg, East Prussia (now called Kaliningrad, and part of the Soviet Union). He spent his whole adult life as a teacher and professor, writing and lecturing on a wide range of subjects, including the natural sciences. Though he never traveled more than forty miles from his hometown, he took a lively interest in the outside world and kept well informed. His moral and political ideas were influenced by the writings of Jean-Jacques Rousseau and by the democratic revolutions in France and the United States, both of which occurred during his lifetime. Though his moral philosophy is abstract and difficult, it is meant to provide a foundation for the concrete ideal of respect for individual persons that seemed to underlie the liberal political movements of his day.

For philosophers like Aristotle, the basic question of ethics was how an individual should live his or her life, and it was assumed that that question was to be understood as being about what is good for the individual. For Kant, and indeed for all philosophers from the seventeenth century on, morality is largely a matter of *duty*, and questions about duties are mainly questions about how one should conduct oneself in one's relations with others. A large part of morality, so conceived, has to do with the arrangements, the systems of rights and obligations, that structure interpersonal relationships. But questions about social arrangements and about how people should relate to one another cannot be answered simply by knowing what is good for any one person. They must be answered from some more detached, disinterested, or impartial standpoint. Accordingly, we can say that a basic difference between the moral philosophy of ancient Greece and that of the modern period is in their conceptions of the *standpoint* from which moral questions are to be resolved. In the modern view, when one reasons morally, one does not reason just in terms of one's own good. When one acts morally, one does not act out of self-interest. Morality may have a point or purpose, but the purpose of moral action is surely not just the purpose of promoting the agent's own good.

All of these ideas figure prominently in Kant's work. In particular, according to him, the distinction between morally good action and self-interested action, between moral rules and rules of self-interest, is absolutely essential to understanding the nature of morality. To say that the moral standpoint is different from a single individual's standpoint, however, is not to say *which* distinct standpoint it is. Kant and other modern philosophers do not agree on the answer. In his most widely read book, *Grounding for the Metaphysics of Morals*,[1] Kant attempts to defend a particular account of the moral standpoint, of the nature of the requirements of morality, and of the source of their authority.

MORAL LAWS AND MORAL ACTION

In the preface to the *Grounding*, Kant speaks of morality in terms of moral *laws*. He wishes to work out a "pure moral philosophy," a moral philosophy that makes sense of "the common idea of duty and of moral laws." According to this common idea, he thinks, a law that is morally valid "must carry with it absolute necessity" and must apply to all rational beings [389]. Yet these laws are to be distinguished from laws of nature, that is, laws of the kind the natural sciences discover. The latter are laws "according to which everything does happen," while moral laws, which he also calls "laws of freedom," are laws "according to which everything ought to happen" [387-388]. Kant begins his investigation of morality in the first section, however, not by discussing moral laws directly but by discussing the nature of morally good *action*.

According to Kant, nothing in the world is "good without qualification," except for "a *good will*." Other "talents of the mind" and "qualities of temperament" of the kind Aristotle and Epictetus valued (Kant mentions wit, judgment, courage, moderation in emotions and passions, and self-control, among others) are good in some respects, he says, but they have no "unconditional worth." Only a good will has that [393-394]. As I understand Kant, he thinks of these judgments as judgments his readers will find perfectly natural. They are a fundamental part of the moral outlook he shares with his readers. What he believes is that when we look carefully at what a good will is, at what acting with a good will involves, we will be led to understand the essential nature of morality. What, then, is it like to act with a good will?

When *we* speak of a man of goodwill, we probably think of someone who is kind and generous, charitable in his judgments of others and anxious to cooperate. But Kant does not think of a morally good will in these terms. In order to understand what it is like to have or to act from a good will, Kant says, we must begin with the concept of "duty" [397]. The idea, evidently, is that when people act with a good will, they act *from duty*. But what does acting from duty amount to? When people act from duty, they do what morality requires (refrain from cheating customers, help others in need), but they do not do it because they think it will promote some further goal they seek. They do not even act from a direct inclination, like a direct benevolent concern for the welfare of others [397-398]. People who act with a good will act "not from inclination, but from duty" [399]. Acting with a good will then, is inconsistent with acting from any inclination.

In addition, Kant says, acting with a good will is good in itself, regardless of whether one actually succeeds in achieving the purpose one intended to achieve [399, cf. 394]. Thus, while acting with a good will is acting from duty, acting from duty is not a matter of actually achieving some purpose (like successfully alleviating the distress of someone in need). Instead, acting from duty is (just) a matter of acting in a way necessitated by respect for the moral law [400-401]. We might put it this way: A person who acts with a good will, a person whose actions have unconditional worth, is a person who endeavors to do what is right, *just* because it is required by the moral law. Such people act, as we might say, purely on principle and not as a result of any desire.

Both parts of this are important. A person who acts, say, on the principle of not telling a lie, but who acts on this principle because she hopes to gain the trust of others, is acting on an inclination and so is not acting from duty. Indeed, even someone who has the virtue of truthfulness, as Aristotle might understand it--a person who has acquired an aversion to lying itself and so has a desire not to lie and acts on it--is not acting with a good will as Kant understands this. A person who acts with a good will acts on a moral law, but on *no* inclination, not even a direct one.

This idea creates a puzzle for Kant:

> What sort of law can that be the thought of which must determine the will without reference to any expected effect, so that the will can be called absolutely good without qualification? Since I have deprived the will of every impulse that might arise for it from obeying any particular law, there is nothing left to serve the will as principle except the universal conformity of its actions to law as such, i.e., I should

never act except in such a way that I can also will that my maxim
should become a universal law [402].

When we act with a good will, Kant is saying, the only motive for our
action, the only explanation for what we do, is that the act is required
by a moral principle. But how can that fact by itself explain our acting
as we do? Kant apparently thinks that any ordinary moral principle,
like "don't lie" or "treat people fairly," cannot in itself be a person's
only reason for acting. If that is one's principle, then one must be acting
on it in part because one also has some inclination, direct or indirect,
that leads one to care about acting on the principle. What he concludes,
in the above passage, is that there is only one principle that can
motivate an action independent of any inclination. That principle says
one must always act in such a way that one can will one's maxim (the
specific principle on which one acts) to be a universal law.
     I will call this principle the "Universalization Principle." In my
judgment, Kant fails to show that, in fact, this is the only principle one
could be acting on if one is acting with a good will. (He does not propose
or consider alternatives.) However, I will put this objection to one side.
The Universalization Principle is philosophically interesting in its
own right. For one thing, it seems to embody an interesting conception of
the distinctive standpoint of morality, and I will have a good deal to
say about it subsequently. For the moment, however, I shall focus on the
main line of Kant's argument. For, *if* Kant had indeed shown that the
Universalization Principle is the principle on which one must be acting
if one acts with a good will, and *if* he were right that acting morally is
acting with a good will, he would have shown that anyone who ever
acts morally acts on this principle.
     There are two big "ifs" here; but assuming for the moment that Kant
is right, further consequences follow. One consequence is that it is very
difficult ever to *know* whether someone is acting with a morally good
will: "We meet frequent and--as we ourselves admit--justified
complaints that there cannot be cited a single certain example of the
disposition to act from pure duty" [406]. "It is indeed sometimes the
case . . . that we can find nothing except the moral ground of duty that
could have been strong enough to move us to this or that good action . . .
[b]ut there cannot with certainty be at all inferred from this that some
secret impulse of self-love, merely appearing as the idea of duty, was
not the actual determining cause of the will" [407].
     If Kant is right, an essential part of our idea of morality is that
people act morally--with a good will--only when their actions are not
based on any desire or inclination. They must be acting *simply* in
obedience to some law and *just* because that law requires them so to act.
But since it is hard to know whether some inclination plays even a

small role in a decision to act, we never know for sure whether a person acts with a good will.

In order to sharpen and clarify this point, Kant formulates a distinction between two different kinds of law that apply to people. Human beings, like other things in nature, are subject to laws. Some laws, like the law of gravity, we "obey" automatically. No one bothers to say that we *ought* to obey this law. We just do. Laws of physics, chemistry, and biology determine what we do because we are physical bodies. We are not, however, *just* physical bodies. We also have a rational nature, and how we behave is determined partly by the laws of reason. As Kant sees it, laws of reason, which include laws of logic (good reasoning) and also moral laws and laws of rational choice and action generally, govern the behavior of rational creatures just as laws of physics or chemistry govern the behavior of physical bodies.

Though we are rational creatures, and so tend to behave as reason requires, we are not perfectly rational. While laws of reason sometimes help determine how we behave--while they sometimes explain what we do--the forces of reason are not always sufficiently strong to guarantee that we think or act rationally. Laws like laws of reason or morality, the consciousness of which can determine how we act but which do not do so automatically, Kant calls "imperatives." And imperatives, he says, are expressed by the term "ought" [412-413]. While we don't say that people *ought* to obey laws of gravity, we do say that they *ought* to be moral or that they ought to reason validly.

There are, Kant goes on to say, two kinds of imperative: hypothetical imperatives and categorical imperatives. What is the difference? Hypothetical imperatives "represent the practical necessity of a possible action as a means for attaining something else that one wants (or may possibly want). The categorical imperative would be one that represented an action as objectively necessary in itself, without reference to another end" [414]. To put it another way, hypothetical imperatives tell us how to behave rationally in the pursuit of some independently given end or goal; categorical imperatives tell us what is rationally required, whatever goals we have or do not have.

Imperatives are expressed by the word "ought." When an imperative applies to someone, we say there is something the person ought to do. Part of what Kant means when he says that some ought-judgments are hypothetical and some categorical is that what makes hypothetical oughts true or false is different from what makes categorical oughts true or false. Suppose I say to my daughter that she ought to take out the garbage. Is it true that she ought to do so? Well, if the imperative is (merely) hypothetical, then it is true that she ought to take out the garbage *only if her doing so is necessary for her because of something she wants.* (Perhaps she will get her allowance only if she takes out the garbage.) If it turns out she does not want her allowance or that she can get it without taking out the garbage, then the hypothetical ought-judgment would be false. If the imperative is categorical, on the other hand, then it is true *even if her taking out the garbage satisfies no desire or inclination she has.* Categorical imperatives, when they are true, are true regardless of the desires or inclinations of those to whom they apply. Hypothetical imperatives, as Kant says later, are "contingent." They "can always be ignored once the purpose is abandoned" [420]. Categorical imperatives, by contrast, are *inescapable*.

The laws and imperatives of morality must be categorical, if Kant is correct. It is easy to see why he has to believe this, given the rest of his theory. According to Kant, when one acts morally, with a good will, one acts on a moral law but not on a desire or inclination. But notice that if one were acting on a mere hypothetical imperative, an essential part of one's reason for acting *would* be some desire or inclination. That is because hypothetical imperatives apply to people only when they have a desire that is satisfied by acting on the imperative. Hence, moral laws must apply categorically, not hypothetically. And on this point many modern philosophers, even when they reject the rest of what Kant says, agree. It is almost a commonplace that, if a moral judgment is true--if it is true, for example, that we morally ought not to steal or cheat--it is true regardless of whether we *want* something that we get by obeying these rules.

Having formulated the distinction between hypothetical and categorical imperatives, Kant next asks how categorical imperatives are *possible* [419]. This is a hard question for Kant because, as he understands the idea of a categorical imperative, it is not just an imperative that is true, regardless of the agent's desires. It is also an imperative that the agent is not free to ignore: If a categorical imperative applies to me, then I must have an inescapable reason to do what it requires, and this reason must also be the kind of reason that motivates me to act and could serve to explain how I act as I do. What concerns Kant is how there could be imperatives, or laws, that explain, all by themselves, a person's acting a certain way. The real question is how moral *action*, understood as action motivated by a categorical imperative, is possible. How can a categorical moral law be a motivating reason for a person's action in the same way that the law of gravity is the reason for an object's falling to earth?

When we explain an action, the explanation usually has at least two parts: Why did Alfred put money in the soft drink machine? Because he wanted a cold drink *and* because he thought that, if one wants a cold drink, one ought to put money in a soft drink machine. If he hadn't believed this, or something like it, then no matter how thirsty he was, that wouldn't have explained putting the money in the machine. Thirst, by itself, doesn't explain putting quarters in slots. The hypothetical imperative, "if one wants a soft drink, one ought to . . .," is part of the explanation, too. But then, this imperative cannot explain the action all by itself, either. The general rule helps explain the action only if there is also a desire for a cold drink. That, again, is why hypothetical imperatives cannot be the basis for *moral* action, as Kant understands it; for moral action is not even partly based on desires.

The problem Kant means to address when he asks how categorical imperatives are possible is the problem of explaining how some imperatives--the categorical ones--can explain action all by themselves. How is it possible that someone does something, for example, helps someone in need or refrains from cheating on a test, and does it *just* because the moral law requires it, and not because he or she has an independent desire to do it?

This is equivalent to the question of whether anyone ever *could* act with a good will. As Kant himself says in a passage I quoted, we cannot find out whether such action is possible by observing others or even ourselves. Someone may appear to be motivated solely by a categorical demand of morality, but it is always possible that there is some independent desire or inclination, hidden perhaps even from the agent himself.

Kant's own idea (which he does not justify independently) is that the categorical imperatives of morality apply to us because they are requirements of reason. Like rules of logic, they tell us what we need to do to be rational. Since all categorical imperatives derive from one basic one, the one he formulated as the Universalization Principle, and since this principle is a principle of reason, he concludes that we must follow this principle if we are to be rational. But since we are naturally rational creatures in part, we are to some extent motivated naturally to do what this and other principles of reason require. If we were purely rational creatures, we would follow laws of reason as automatically as we "follow" the law of gravity. (They wouldn't be imperatives, or "oughts," for us.) We aren't perfectly rational, though, and so we don't always act rationally (or morally). Still, when we do so, we are following our rational nature. Reason is in charge.

Acting on categorical imperatives is possible, then, according to Kant, because these imperatives are laws of reason and because, as rational creatures, it is natural for us to follow such laws. And this leads Kant to a further interesting idea. He thinks of our rational nature as our *real* nature, our essential nature, and he proposes that we act *freely* only when we act according to our real nature. But we act fully rationally only when we follow all laws of reason, and we do this only when we follow moral laws. Hence, we are fully free only when we act morally. Thus, to be free, we must rise above our nature as creatures of inclination and let our behavior be determined by rational and moral principles. The laws of morality, as he says in the preface, are laws of freedom. By acting morally, we realize our nature as free and rational beings. (Here Kant echoes, in an interesting way, the Stoic idea, found in the work of Epictetus, that the ethical life is a life of freedom. By following Stoic teachings, we avoid being dominated either by external events or by our own emotions. We *choose* how we will respond to events.)

Moral action is possible, as Kant conceives it, only if it is possible that we sometimes act as we do just *because reason requires it.* Is this possible? Does reason ever explain our conduct? It has been said, most notoriously by the Scottish philosopher David Hume (1711-1776), that reason alone has no power to influence conduct. "Reason," Hume said, "is, and ought only to be the slave of the passions."[2] Remember the example of Alfred and the soft drink machine. Reason tells us what we have to do to get a drink, but it leads us to put money in the machine only if we are also thirsty. According to Hume, all explanations of action involve a desire in this way.

But there is reason to disagree with Hume. It seems to me perfectly clear that reason can play an explanatory role in our lives. It can certainly explain mental activity like coming to believe, or not to believe, something. We think, for example, that we can explain a person's abandoning a certain belief simply by discovering that it is inconsistent with his or her other beliefs. Similarly, we explain someone's adopting a belief simply on the ground that it follows logically from other beliefs he or she has. The "mere" fact that laws of logic require a belief, given other beliefs, explains someone's having that belief. And though philosophers like Hume tend to emphasize the idea that reason *alone* never explains action, the other side of their theory is that laws of reason play a significant role in motivating and explaining our action, too. People follow rational strategies in deciding what to do. They seem to be influenced, for example, by variations in probabilities and in the size of possible gains and losses in choosing investments or in selecting plays in games like football. In short, in our ordinary thinking about people, we assume they are rational creatures whose actions and beliefs are to be explained at least in part by laws of reason. They tend to follow rules of consistency, of logical inference, and of rational choice.

Suppose we are rational, in the sense that reason at least plays a role in determining our behavior. Does that mean that Kant's problem is solved? Does it show that moral action is possible--that there are categorical imperatives of morality and that people actually act on them, uninfluenced by prior inclinations? Hardly. Perhaps it points in the direction of a solution, but it does not provide one. In the preceding paragraph I assumed, without argument, that requirements of consistency, for example, are requirements of reason. Perhaps it is hard to disagree with that, but it cannot be assumed, without argument, that what we, or Kant, consider to be ordinary rules of morality are also requirements of reason. Kant happens to believe that these ordinary rules can be derived from his general Universalization Principle, so, if that is a principle of reason, the other moral rules are too. But is the Universalization Principle a principle of reason in the same way that the laws of logic are? Philosophers have tried to show that it is, but whether they have succeeded is controversial, to say the least. And even if it is, there would remain the question of whether it is ever sufficient to motivate action.

Before we conclude this section, it is worth considering what bearing these ideas might have on the underlying question of this book. On the one hand, if Kant is right, then it is no part of the point of morality to promote the satisfaction of our independent desires. If we understand the question "why be moral?" as "what's in it for me?" then the most natural answer is "nothing." On the other hand, though, it is Kant's whole idea that if there is such a thing as morality, then we all have a kind of reason to be moral; for the requirements of morality just *are* the requirements of reason. Indeed, in the picture Kant paints, by acting morally we not only choose to be rational, but we also achieve the only genuine freedom. We allow our lives to be governed by reason instead of by nonrational inclinations. And, if this does not mean that we live more happily by living morally, it at least puts morality in what must seem, to many, an attractive light.

KANT'S ARGUMENT CRITICIZED

Kant presents us with an elaborate and exciting system of interrelated ideas. He attempts to show that if we begin with a very simple and, in his view, obvious idea about the nature of morally good action, we can show that moral laws must be categorical laws of reason, that being moral and realizing our nature as free and rational beings are identical, and even that the basic principle of morality must be some version of his Universalization Principle. He does not think he has *proved* that there actually are moral laws or that anyone actually does act morally. What he thinks he has shown is what morality must be like, what must be true about it, if there is such a thing. But he is mistaken, even in this conditional conclusion.

The whole argument depends crucially on assumptions Kant makes very early, when he gives his account of the nature of morally good action. He begins, you will recall, with the idea that there is a difference between morally good or praiseworthy action--what he calls acting with a good will--and action that is correct, that accords with moral requirements, but is not done with a good will. Now most people do agree that there is such a difference. Certainly Aristotle agrees. Aristotle also thinks that a person could do what a virtuous person would do without doing it *as* a virtuous person would--that is, without having the virtues. People can tell the truth, for example, only out of fear of being caught, not because they have come to care about the truth and to choose it for its own sake. A truthful person, on the other hand, has a fixed and firm desire to tell the truth, takes pleasure in doing so, and so chooses the truth for its own sake.

Aristotle then, like Kant, accepts the distinction between good and merely correct action. But he makes the distinction in a different way. Hence, we also can accept the distinction without drawing it in the same way Kant does. For Aristotle, the person who has the virtues and acts virtuously is a person who has acquired certain desires and who acts on them. The generous or truthful person, as Aristotle describes him, has what Kant would call a "direct inclination" to share or to tell the truth. For Kant, though, one who acts with a good will acts on no inclination, not even a direct one. This is a crucial difference. For Aristotle, being moral is, in part, a matter of having the *right* inclinations; for Kant, it is a matter of rising *above* inclination, a matter of reason's taking control over our affective nature.

Suppose we agree with *Kant* that morally good or praiseworthy action is different from action that is not morally good, but suppose we adopt something more like *Aristotle's* account of what makes action morally good: People act with a good will when they take a direct interest in doing the right thing, choosing it for its own sake. In that case, a person who acts with a good will is not a person who acts without inclination. But then, we also are not forced to conclude that moral laws are categorical, that they are based on reason alone, or that their motivating force is the force of rationality alone. Finally, even if the Universalization Principle is the only principle that can "determine the will" independent of any prior inclination, we are not forced to conclude that it must be the principle of morality.

It follows that Kant has not demonstrated, on the basis of assumptions that are essential to our very idea of moral action, the main conclusions he wanted to demonstrate concerning the nature of morality. That does not mean these conclusions are false. Perhaps they are true, but for different reasons. I will examine this possibility further in the next section. Here, though, I want to consider the question of *why* Kant makes the assumptions about the good will with which he begins. Why does he assume that people who act with a good will act on no inclination?

Any answer must be, to some extent, speculative; but I suspect Kant came to view the good will as he did for two reasons. First, he makes the assumption, noted at the beginning of this chapter, that the moral standpoint is different from the standpoint of self-interest and, in particular, that moral action is not self-interested action. Second, he believes that any time one acts on an inclination, any time one acts on one of one's own desires, one is acting out of self-interest. Only when we do what reason demands, just because reason demands it and independent of any prior inclination, do we act in a nonself-interested way. Hence, given that morality and self-interest are incompatible, only when we act on *no* inclination do we act morally. How good is this reasoning?

The idea that the ethical life involves some limits on the direct pursuit of immediate self-interest is, in fact, an idea that almost all moral philosophers have accepted. On this point, Kant does not depart from tradition. Indeed, it seems to me clear that Epictetus and Aristotle, though each saw ethics as the study of how one should live in order to have a good life for oneself, both thought that one had to control selfish impulses; and Aristotle in particular thought one had to develop a direct concern for, for example, truth and justice. They saw the fundamental point of morality as the promotion of one's own good, but they thought this required that individual actions *not* be self-interested. As Kant sees it, though, even someone who has and acts out of a direct inclination to do what justice requires is "really" just acting out of self-interest. After all, he is really *just doing what he wants.* Hence, he is not really acting morally.

Who is right here? Should we say that the Aristotelian virtuous person is acting morally since he acts out of a direct desire to do justice and not out of a desire to benefit himself? Or should we say that he really is acting selfishly since he is doing what he wants? Kant's way of thinking about self-interest is very common in contemporary culture. Jeremy Bentham and John Stuart Mill, whom we will discuss in

Chapter 5, both accept it. Indeed, most modern economists accept it, and accept it for a reason like Kant's: They think that people tend to do *what they want*, and they conclude from this that people always act out of self-interest. But, since most modern theorists have rejected Kant's idea that we ever act out of reason alone, they conclude that people can only act out of self-interest. Still, are they right?

What we need, if we are to resolve this dispute, is a clear definition of what it means to act out of self-interest. In the next chapter, I will examine a definition offered by Joseph Butler, together with his argument that it is impossible to act *solely* out of self-interest and that it certainly is possible to act for reasons entirely other than self-interest. What is significant about Butler's account of selfish and unselfish action is that the distinction does not depend on whether one acts on inclination or not. Thus, one could be acting on inclination but still not out of self-interest. Hence, if Butler is right, Kant is wrong, and that means that someone with the Aristotelian virtues would be acting in a moral (i.e., nonself-interested) way. Moreover, it also opens the way for an account of the nature and basis of morality quite different from Kant's, in which the distinction between the moral and nonmoral depends not on reason but on sentiment or emotion. An account like this was offered in the eighteenth century by Hume. His theory will be discussed in the next chapter along with Butler's.

THE CATEGORICAL IMPERATIVE REVISITED

Based on his assumption that people act with a good will only when they act on no inclination, Kant concludes that moral imperatives must be categorical and, also, that there is only one *basic* categorical moral law, namely, the Universalization Principle. This law (which Kant formulates in several different ways) is often called *the* categorical imperative. Kant claims that it is the only law capable of determining the will independent of any prior inclination, though he also thinks additional, more specific imperatives, like the requirement that one not break a promise, can be derived from it. When people act with a good will, they may be directly following specific requirements, like the requirement not to lie. But, if their action is fully moral, they will be acting on that requirement because, in turn, they see that the maxim of not lying is a maxim they can will to be a universal law. Their most basic reason--the reason that "determines the will"--is the Universalization Principle.

If I am correct, Kant is wrong in his original assumption. Acting with a good will does not require acting on no inclination. Therefore,

Kant has not shown that moral imperatives must be categorical nor that *the* categorical imperative is the basic principle of morality. However, even if Kant has not *shown* it, it might still be true that this is the basic principle of morality. Some ethical questions, I have claimed, need to be addressed and answered from a standpoint different from the standpoint of any particular individual. These include, most obviously, questions about what rights people have against other people, what obligations people have to other people, or, more generally, what people must do or refrain from doing when there is a conflict of interest among them. Questions about the extent and limits of property rights, about the fair distribution of the tax burden, about rights to health care, and about the rights and duties of patients and health care professionals are only a few examples. What most philosophers now would say is that, to answer these questions, we need to employ some procedure that is *impartial* among the different persons or interests that are involved. What is interesting is that Kant's Universalization Principle looks, to many people, like the very embodiment of a kind of moral impartiality. So, perhaps it is the principle we ought to employ, even if it is not necessary for the reasons Kant offers.

When we apply the universalization test to a proposed course of action, what we are asking, in effect, is whether we would be prepared to make it a law that anyone faced with similar circumstances act as we propose to act. If we would be unwilling to accept the consequences of others acting as we propose to, we should not do so ourselves. Thus, for example, if we care about some goal or project and if we need the cooperation of others to gain it, the categorical imperative tells us that we cannot exempt ourselves from the requirement of cooperating. It tells us not to demand of others more than we are willing to demand of ourselves. In that sense, it tells us to treat others equally with ourselves. If we would want others to treat us a certain way, it requires that we treat them the same way. Thus, it seems to rule out both certain kinds of "free-riding" and also things like deception, discrimination, and physical violence.

Should we then conclude that Kant's principle is the right principle to use in making moral decisions? There are at least two reasons to resist this conclusion. First, though it appears on first examination that the principle has quite definite consequences and, indeed, that its consequences coincide with obvious moral requirements, under more careful scrutiny it is not clear that it has any definite consequences at all. Second, though it might appear that the principle captures the very essence of the idea of impartiality, it turns out that impartiality can be interpreted in a variety of ways. Kant's principle is not the only impartial principle. Let me explain each of these objections in more detail.

The first objection is that Kant's principle does not, in fact, settle interesting moral questions. Why not? The Universalization Principle is a lot like The Golden Rule, and the problem should really be familiar to anyone who has thought seriously about how this rule is supposed to work. Suppose that a member of my family, someone I love, is suffering from a terminal illness and is no longer able to make decisions rationally or even to understand the real nature of her condition. There is no doubt that she will live a month at most. She is quite uncomfortable and is no longer able to interact socially with friends and family. She can die a quick and peaceful death if certain treatments are stopped. The doctor offers to stop them. Should I agree?

I could ask Kant's question, namely, could I will that everyone act as I propose to act? But just how do I describe my act? If we withdraw the treatment, we kill an innocent person. Could I will that everyone with the opportunity to kill an innocent person do so? On the other hand, if we withdraw the treatment, we end the suffering of a dying person and we help her to die more peacefully. Surely, I can will that, in cases like this, we should help dying people to die peacefully. (I would want it for myself.) But now it seems that Kant's test leads to a different answer depending on how we describe the action we are considering. Both descriptions are true, so which should we choose? Nothing in Kant's theory tells us how to answer this question, and without an answer we cannot use his principle to resolve ethical dilemmas like this one.

Now consider the second objection. Even if we could give an unambiguous interpretation to Kant's principle, it could still be objected that it is not impartial among people *in the right way*. The Universalization Principle requires that we demand the same of ourselves that we demand of others. It requires a kind of consistency. We shouldn't, for example, demand sacrifices of others unless we would demand them of ourselves. But is this the only kind of impartiality that morality requires? Suppose we *would* be willing that others act a certain way. Is this enough to justify our acting in that way? What if we would be willing to have them act that way toward us, but they are not willing that anyone act that way toward them?

The kind of impartiality implicit in the Universalization Principle seems to amount just to a kind of consistency, consistency in the application of our own ideals or preferences to the evaluation of everyone's conduct. If we apply certain standards to the evaluation of what others do, it says that we must apply the same standards to the evaluation of our own conduct. Immorality, in this view, is a kind of hypocrisy. A different idea of impartiality is that, before we decide what to do, we must put ourselves in the position of others. We do not just view our conduct, consistently, from the standpoint of our own values and interests; we consider it from the standpoint of the values and interests of others as well.

Consider an example. I support a variety of environmental causes. I value clean air and clear water; I care about protecting endangered species and unspoiled wilderness. As a result, I want people to make certain sacrifices, to accept limits on their liberty to pollute and otherwise to exploit the land in ways that might be profitable and productive. Applying Kant's Universalization Principle to the evaluation of my own conduct, I accept similar restrictions on my liberty. I try to refrain from activities that pollute, for example, because I would not will that others pollute. I consistently demand from myself the same sacrifices I want from others. (Indeed, I do this even though I realize that if I *alone* polluted, it would do no noticeable damage. My reasoning is not based on consequences alone, but on something like the notion that burdens should be shared fairly.)

Now, imagine someone else who does not care about preserving natural beauty, but who likes, say, riding his motorcycle through fragile mountain meadows. May he do so? If he asks Kant's question, that is, whether he would will that everyone do as he proposes to do, the answer might well be "yes." He has no interest in preserving the meadows. So, for him, it is permissible to destroy them. Is this a reasonable moral conclusion? Perhaps so. Perhaps what is permissible for him is not permissible for me. Perhaps what is permissible for each of us depends on our own commitments and ideals. (Since we all share *some* interests, like an interest in not being maimed or injured, some things are permissible for no one.) But some people might disagree with this conclusion. They might say that morality demands more of the motorcyclist than consistent adherence to his own values. He needs to ask not just what he, with his commitments, could will that everyone do, but instead what other people, with their commitments, could accept, too.

The moral ideal of impartiality, then, might be understood to require more than consistent avoidance of hypocrisy. It might be understood to require that we in some way take account of the interests, values, or viewpoints of others. If morality requires that we act from an impartial standpoint, but there is more than one kind of impartiality, then mere appeal to the idea of impartiality itself does not determine what we must do. As I have said, much of modern moral philosophy consists of disputes about just what kind of impartiality morality demands and about the relative merits of different conceptions of this notion. Utilitarianism, which we will consider in later chapters, can be understood as a systematic development of one particular ideal of impartiality. Before we turn to utilitarianism, however, it is important to recall that Kant himself formulates the categorical imperative, the basic principle of morality, in more than one way; and though he believes that they are all equivalent, they actually, at the very least, convey rather different images of moral reasoning.

I will focus on two formulations. In the second section of the *Grounding*, Kant formulates the imperative as follows: "Act in such a way that you treat humanity, whether in your own person or in the person of another, always at the same time as an end and never simply as a means" [429]. This, Kant says, is the "supreme limiting condition of every man's freedom of action" [431]. Moral people not only limit their actions to those they are willing that others do as well, they also refrain from using others as means to their own ends. Moreover, Kant makes clear at this point, morality is not a matter of just avoiding what one cannot will universally; it is a matter of following obligatory *laws*, but laws one wills oneself as universal laws consistent with the demands of reason, including the "supreme limiting condition" [431]. People are both creators of the moral law (when they "legislate" in accordance with the requirements of reason) and they are also the people to whom the laws apply. This thought leads Kant to the further idea of what he calls "a kingdom of ends," "a systematic union of rational beings through common objective laws" [433].

Admittedly, it is hard to know just what to make of these rather heady ideas, but one possible interpretation is this: People act morally when and only when they obey laws or rules, in their dealings with one another, which *all* of them would be willing to accept as universally binding. In obeying these laws that all could will, they would each be acting as both sovereign and subject. Each would act in a way consistent with rules he or she would be willing to have universally followed, and since each would also be following laws the *others* would be willing to accept, each could be said to be treating the others as ends, not merely as means. What any one does can be justified *to* the others for it is consistent with rules each can agree to. Morality, viewed this way, is a kind of agreement, though an ideal or hypothetical agreement, not an actual one.

It needs to be emphasized that this is not something Kant says explicitly in the *Grounding*. I claim only to have drawn a picture of an idea of morality suggested by Kant's remarks. Regardless of whether Kant would endorse this idea, however, it is an intriguing one and one that many twentieth-century philosophers in the so-called "social contract" tradition have found attractive. There are a number of versions of this idea, and this is not the place to try to describe the different possibilities. (I will discuss one variation in Chapter 6.) I mention it now for two reasons. First, if the moral standpoint is the impartial standpoint, one interpretation of this idea is that it requires us to act in a way that can be justified to everyone in terms of principles each can accept. This idea contrasts, I will later argue, with the idea of impartiality implicit in the moral philosophy of utilitarianism. Second, in its emphasis on what is justifiable *to each*, it embodies a possible interpretation of the Kantian injunction to treat everyone as an end, and so it can be said to be inspired by Kant.

CONCLUSION: ANCIENT AND MODERN

Epictetus and Aristotle thought that the attitudes and character traits they advocated were good for their possessors. They thought that these traits, including, in the case of Aristotle, moral virtues like generosity and justice, contributed to one's own happiness. Indeed, it is fair to say that, for them, the study of ethics just is the study of the kind of upbringing and character one needs to achieve well-being.

Kant, together with most other modern moral philosophers, does not view morality in this way. For modern philosophers, the restrictions of morality are meant to serve the needs or purposes of people generally, where these needs and purposes are assessed from an impartial standpoint. If it is not the *aim* of moral requirements to advance the good of the agent who acts on them, however, then what reason does he or she have to respect them at all? How this question can be answered is, of course, the overarching theme of this book. For an Aristotelian, the question might arise at either of two levels. If the question is what reason people have to do particular acts that are virtuous, the answer is that, if they have the virtues, they will have acquired a direct interest in acting virtuously. They will simply want to. On another level, though, if the question is whether people (were they in a position to make this choice) would have a reason to acquire the virtues in the first place, the answer is that having the virtues is in one's own interest: They help make possible a kind of life that is likely to be good. And, for the same reason, parents who care about their children have a good reason to teach them the virtues. But how might someone who sees morality as Kant sees it answer the same question?

Kant's own answer is, in a way, very simple. We are, to some extent, naturally rational creatures, and that means that we are naturally governed by the requirements of reason--we naturally tend to think and choose in accordance with reason. The demand that we be impartial, Kant thinks, is itself a demand that our own reason makes on us. As rational creatures, we just *do* care about being impartial, in the same way that, as rational creatures, we just *do* strive to keep our beliefs consistent. As *imperfect* rational individuals, affected by irrational strivings and inclinations, we experience reason's requirements as demands, and we do not always heed them. Nevertheless, it is as natural for us to follow reason as it is for us to follow our inclinations.

While I do not deny that humans are rational and that their behavior is partly governed by what can be thought of as laws of reason, I am not convinced that Kant's categorical imperative, in any of its versions, is itself a law of reason. We cannot assume, then, that all rational human beings, just because they naturally strive to follow reason, naturally aim to obey the categorical imperative. Many people may in fact have reason to follow some such moral law but, if they do, it will be because they have some desire or concern that gives them an interest in doing so. Philosophers like Hume and Butler, whom I will discuss in the next chapter, think people *naturally* have kind and generous desires that lead them to behave as impartial morality requires. Others, more like Aristotle, think that these desires arise out of one's upbringing. Either way, though, these reasons are what Kant would call "inclinations." But as far as I can see, Kant gives us no convincing reason to believe that our reasons for being moral are, or must be, anything but inclinations.

There is some parallel here with what I said about Aristotle. Aristotle believed that the virtues contributed to a happy life and, thus, that they could be justified to anyone who cared about leading a happy life. I argued that this conclusion needs to be qualified. At the very least, it is not true that all the virtues are *necessary* for a good life; and vices can, in some cases, be useful. Still, I argued that the virtues are compatible with a happy life and that they definitely improve the quality of many good lives. In that sense, they can be justified to many people, indeed to most, given normal aims and purposes. Perhaps that is all that Aristotle ever intended to claim. Kant meant to claim more. He wished to show that the demands of morality were inescapable, not only in the sense that moral laws apply to people independent of their desires or inclinations but also in the sense that everyone, necessarily, has a reason to act on them. I don't believe Kant succeeded in showing this.

Kant's claim is a large one. People who care about morality, who even make substantial sacrifices for what they see as moral causes, may very much want to *believe* that they have no rational alternative. They may very much want to believe that those who ignore morality, with seeming impunity, are really irrational by their own standards. They may want to believe that there are arguments for being moral that even immoral scoundrels could not reject if only they really listened. This is the kind of claim Kant is making. But, again, he has not established it.[3]

If I am right, then we have reasons to be moral, as Kant understands morality, only if we have certain contingent aims or purposes. Once we grant that, then the interesting questions are "what kinds of aim or attitude would lead us to be concerned with the requirements of Kantian morality?" "how prevalent are these attitudes?" and "how do they fit into a good human life?" Here is a brief sketch of a possible answer.

Kantian morality requires that we comply with certain principles, principles that apply to everyone and that are acceptable, as principles applying to everyone, from the point of view of each. When we act on such principles, we treat each person as an end, even if we act contrary to someone's particular interest, for we act on a principle each would agree to as a principle for everyone. Now, there will be situations in which a person would benefit, in terms of plain self-interest, by not following a policy he or she would want everyone else to follow. (If everyone else contributed to public television, for example, I could enjoy the shows, even if I did not contribute.) And there will certainly be situations in which the universal principles one person favors will not be the same ones others could accept. (I might favor total prohibition of motorcycles anywhere but on roads. That may be unacceptable to others.) But people who advocate one policy for others and do not follow it themselves are at least hypocrites, taking advantage of the cooperation of others; and people who refuse, in deciding what to do themselves, even to consider what others might find acceptable, run a risk of not being able to defend their actions to others by any arguments that are likely to be compelling.

Some people, no doubt, are quite indifferent to the opinions of others. They do not care if others think them to be hypocrites. However, people who do want to live on good terms with others, who do not want to have to lie and conceal, and who want to be able to justify what they do when challenged, do have a good reason to care about morality as Kant conceives it.[4] And perhaps those of us who share these attitudes also have a good reason to be wary of those who do not. In a community in which most people do want to live openly and in good faith with each other, someone who seeks the pleasures of social life has good reason to adopt similar attitudes. Moreover, if the pleasures of social life are a significant part of human good, then an

Aristotelian would advocate that people acquire a disposition to act as they need to in order to be able to live openly with others. And that may mean that they would have to follow something like the requirements of Kantian morality. It is an intriguing thought that the virtue of justice, as it can be justified by an Aristotelian argument, might involve a disposition to act as Kant would require--to follow something like the categorical imperative. We could put the point this way: Kant may be wrong about the nature and foundation of morality, and Aristotle may be right. But what morality as Aristotle conceives it *requires* may be in part what Kant thinks it requires.

4

SELF-INTEREST, ALTRUISM, AND SOCIAL CONVENTIONS

THOMAS HOBBES, 1588-1679
DAVID HUME, 1711-1776
JOSEPH BUTLER, 1692-1752

Kant, on the one hand, and Aristotle and Epictetus, on the other, seem to have quite different pictures of what ethics is about. For the Greeks, ethics attempts to answer the very general question "how should one live one's life?" and it assumes that this is a question about how one should live in order to live well and be happy. According to Kant, though, the demands of morality are not in any way based on what contributes to the agent's own well-being. They are demands of an impartial practical reason. They tell us to follow rules that are rationally acceptable not just to the agent but to anyone. And, as a consequence, Kantian morality is concerned more directly with the good of others than with the good of the agent.

Of the three philosophers discussed in this chapter, two, David Hume and Joseph Butler, were rough contemporaries of Kant and the third, Thomas Hobbes, lived only a century earlier. All of them have a conception of morality more like Kant's than like that of the Greeks: Morality limits our pursuit of our own self-interest; it requires that we cooperate with others, that we consider their interests as well as our own, and that we sometimes go out of our way just to promote their good. Also, like Kant, each of these philosophers believes people are, to a significant extent, naturally motivated by self-interest. Given that we are naturally self-interested, but that morality requires limits on the pursuit of self-interest, a central question for each, as for Kant, is how morality is *possible*: How is it possible that people act morally? How is it that people are motivated to care about morality or, even, how do they come to conceive of the idea of morality?

Kant answered these questions by postulating that moral laws are laws of reason that motivate rational beings independent of inclinations, which he sees as self-interested. According to Kant, when people act morally--when they act with a good will--they are simply doing what their own reason requires. Hobbes, Hume, and Butler, however, do not make this assumption. They attempt to account for and justify morality in terms of a more ordinary, mundane conception of human motives. Their project is the subject of this chapter. If they are correct, then despite what Kant says, our natural inclinations actually do provide us with adequate motivation and justification for acting as morality requires.

HUME ON THE NATURE AND SOURCE OF MORAL REQUIREMENTS

David Hume, perhaps the most important and influential philosopher in the British empiricist tradition, was born in Edinburgh, Scotland, in 1711. His overriding aim, in all areas of philosophy, was to offer an account of philosophical facts consistent with the world view of the natural sciences and free from controversial metaphysical or religious assumptions. My exposition of Hume's moral views will be based on his *Enquiry Concerning the Principles of Morals*,[1] a reworking of Part III of *A Treatise of Human Nature*,[2] published twelve years earlier.

Some people, Hume notes at the beginning of his *Enquiry*, deny the reality of "moral distinctions." They deny that some things are good, some bad, some right, and some wrong. But such people, he says, do not deserve to be taken seriously. They may *say* there is no such thing as a good or bad act or motive when they are talking philosophy, but if they are asked a real question about a real person, they will have no trouble listing his good or bad traits. Indeed, Hume says, not only do people, in practice, speak and act as if moral distinctions are real, they also, to a large extent, agree with one another about which actions or motives are good and which bad.

If Hume is right, then, it is silly to spend much time on the question of whether there really are good or bad people. If we are honest with ourselves, we all think there are. But, Hume says, "There is another controversy . . . much better worth examination, concerning the general foundation of morals" [13]. This controversy is about what moral distinctions, or moral ideas, are *based on*, what they derive from, or how we come to make such distinctions [13]. This, of course, corresponds to Kant's question of how morality is possible. Also, for Hume, as for

Kant, it is the question whether our moral ideas have an explanation that makes it clear why they are important and need to be taken seriously.

When Hume wrote his *Treatise of Human Nature*, he subtitled it "An Attempt to introduce the experimental Method of Reasoning into Moral Subjects." In the *Enquiry*, he says again that we need to approach our topic "by following the experimental method" [16]. This requires us to proceed in two stages. Before we can expect to figure out what our moral ideas are based on or how we could have come to have such ideas, it seems obvious to Hume that we need to give a systematic account of what those ideas are, and this is the task that will occupy us for several pages. Hume misleadingly describes this as finding out what the "origin" of morality is. But what he means by this is that we need to look at the various kinds of things that are morally good in order to find out what they have in common [16]. It is just as if we knew which animals are called reptiles but didn't know the definition of "reptile." Presumably, we could begin to find the answer by looking to see what the different species of reptile have in common. (Remember, Hume thinks that there is close to universal agreement about what is morally good [16]. If we ask ourselves, honestly, what we would say about someone if we want to praise him--if we are to deliver a eulogy at his funeral, for example--we will find considerable agreement as to what we should or should not say.)

In the course of the *Enquiry*, Hume describes a number of different motives and character traits that people generally consider admirable. The first two he considers, and the two that are arguably of most interest for moral theory, are those of benevolence and justice. Whether these are both morally good, again, is not at issue for Hume. He thinks we all agree they are. His question is what it is about them that *makes* them good, and that, he thinks, is the question of what they have in common.

Hume takes up benevolence in Section II. He notes at the beginning that there are many forms of benevolence, many attitudes or motives that are thought of as benevolent ones [17]. Thus, we say people are benevolent if they are humane, merciful, grateful, friendly, generous, or beneficent. These qualities, Hume thinks, are among the best qualities a person can have: "No qualities are more intitled to the general good-will and approbation of mankind than benevolence and humanity, friendship and gratitude, natural affection and public spirit, or whatever proceeds from a tender sympathy with others, and a generous concern for our kind and species" [18]. But what is it that *makes* these qualities morally good? What is it they have in common? Hume's answer is that these "social virtues" all have what he calls "utility"

[18].   And by that he means that they result in "happiness and satisfaction." "[T]hey all have a "tendency to promote the interests of our species, and bestow happiness on human society" [18, 20]. He concludes that utility, or the tendency to produce happiness for people, is at least in part what moral goodness consists of. It is what an action or motive must have if it is to be a good one. Or, to put the same point differently, when we say that benevolent attitudes and actions are good, what we are saying is that they tend to promote happiness.

We can think of Hume's idea here--his idea that morality or moral goodness is a matter of utility--as a somewhat tentative hypothesis. It is a hypothesis he formulates after considering just one group of moral attitudes, namely, the attitudes characteristic of benevolence. The question he is left with at the end of Section II is whether the tendency to promote happiness is the element common to other kinds of morally good motive or action as well; and with that question in mind, he takes up in Section III the case of justice.

We might expect that justice would present a particularly difficult problem for Hume's hypothesis. After all, it is not surprising that benevolent actions and attitudes would tend to advance people's happiness and well-being. Benevolence is, by definition, a disposition to do good or to wish others well. But justice at least seems like a very different matter. The just person doesn't so much aim to do good but, rather, to give what is deserved, to treat people fairly and to respect their rights. Indeed, sometimes, what is deserved is punishment or a rebuke; so giving people what they deserve is not always the sort of thing one does out of benevolence. Moreover, even when we are talking about prizes or rewards, the just person gives the prize not to the person it will most benefit, but to the person who deserves it or won it in a fair competition. And the same is true if we have in mind respect for rights instead of desert. In an appendix, "Some farther Considerations with regard to Justice," Hume himself observes that "regard to the particular right of one individual citizen may . . . be productive of pernicious consequences . . . may be extremely hurtful." He gives the example of a bad man who will misuse his fortune but who is rightfully entitled to it because he inherited it [94]. Indeed, many of the problems discussed in fields like medical ethics seem to involve *conflicts* between what would appear to be the best course of action in terms of a benevolent concern for a patient's welfare and what seems to be required by respect for the rights either of patients or of health-care professionals.

If this is right, then, when we look at particular examples of just acts, we should not expect to find that they all have in common a tendency to promote human happiness. Sometimes, what justice requires is that we do or permit something that is actually harmful. And this suggests that Hume's hypothesis--the hypothesis that morally good things are all things that promote happiness--is mistaken. Surprisingly, though, Hume does not draw this conclusion. He actually thinks the case of justice confirms his hypothesis that what is morally good is what promotes happiness. How does he arrive at this conclusion?

When he discusses justice in Section III, he does not proceed by examining individual examples of just acts, or even kinds of just act. He proceeds indirectly, by describing a number of different "science fiction" worlds. The first is a sort of Garden of Eden--a world in which there is a superabundance of food and other external goods. The second is a world in which there is normal scarcity, but in which people are supergenerous and everyone is willing to share anything others need more. And then Hume changes the examples by considering a world in which scarcity is so great that no beneficial cooperation is possible at all and a world in which people are so vicious or cruel that a decent person needs to use any means available just to survive. What Hume thinks, and expects us to agree with, is that in each of these situations *there is no such thing as justice or injustice.* He is clearly thinking of justice--what he calls "the cautious, jealous virtue of justice" [21]-- mainly as a tendency to respect rights, and especially rights of property. What he expects us to agree with is that, in these worlds, there would be no property rights; and there would be no property rights because, in some sense, they would do no good or serve no purpose in terms of human well-being. Contrariwise, in the normal situation of humankind, where there are rights and requirements of justice, those rights contribute to our well-being and happiness. Necessary goods are sufficiently abundant that individuals can expect to be able to acquire some property; people are sufficiently disciplined that they can expect one another to respect property rights; but there is not such great abundance that people have no need to plan carefully and hang on to what they have. In the words of the twentieth-century philosopher John Rawls, who borrows this idea from Hume, justice becomes an issue when "cooperation is both possible and necessary."[3]

What Hume says here is controversial, and I would not expect all readers to agree with all of it. I myself am pretty much convinced by the Garden of Eden example. It seems to me that, if there could be a world in which whatever a person wanted was there just for the taking and nothing ever ran out, we would not bother to think in terms of *mine* or *yours.* We would not have the idea of property and so would not think of justice in the sense of respect for property rights. Nobody would benefit in any way from rules of property. I am less convinced, however, by some of the other examples. Consider the case in which he imagines a decent person who has fallen into a "society of ruffians" [23]. He says that the decent person would feel no obligation of justice to the ruffians, since it would do *him* no good. But that does not mean it would not help the ruffians, so justice would not be totally useless to everyone in this world. Again, he imagines a world in which there is a species of creature living among us which is greatly inferior, both mentally and physically; and he thinks we would consider these creatures as having no rights [25-26]. Again, though, it seems to me that the inferior creatures would certainly benefit from our thinking of them as having rights, even if *we* would not. Animal rights advocates today would certainly emphasize this point.

What is Hume thinking here? Evidently, he believes, and expects us to agree, that there are requirements of justice only when they benefit not just someone but *everyone*. Rules of justice, as he sees them, represent *something like* an agreement--they are restrictions or requirements people would all accept because each is better off with the restrictions than with no agreement at all. That is why creatures superior in strength and guile owe no duties of justice to inferior creatures. Even though the latter would gain from the rules, the former would not.

We might find ourselves disagreeing with Hume on this point. We might think that even the very weak have *some* rights against the strong. If so, we would have reason to doubt part of Hume's idea about the role of justice in our lives. But I want to leave this question about the details of Hume's account of justice to one side for the moment. Whether or not we think that requirements of justice must be beneficial to *everyone* subject to them, Hume at least thinks he has convinced us that they exist only when they are beneficial to *someone*. Thus, he thinks, he has further confirmed his hypothesis that morality is based on utility--that the common element in the requirements of morality is its tendency to promote human well-being.

The first part of Hume's two-part project of understanding the nature and basis of morality was to give an account of what morality consists of; and his answer was that moral virtues and actions are all, in some way, beneficial. Now we come to the second question: How can we explain the fact that people take an interest in moral requirements, that they praise and admire what is morally good, and that they are motivated to do what they consider to be morally good or right? This is the question he addresses in Section V, "Why Utility Pleases" [38f]. He considers three possible explanations. The first is that our interest in morality is to be explained entirely in terms of social training. But Hume thinks this cannot be the whole story. It simply pushes the question one step further back: Where did the educators themselves get their interest in morality? The second possible explanation is that self-interest leads us to be interested in morality. Hume takes this explanation more seriously but, again, he finds it inadequate. It is true, he thinks, that what is morally good often coincides with what is in our self-interest, but he is struck by the fact that we sometimes find ourselves admiring, praising, and caring about morally good actions and character traits even when our interests aren't involved. We find "instances in which private interest [is] separate from public; in which it [is] even contrary: and yet we [observe] the moral sentiment to continue . . ." [42-43]. Morally good acts and attitudes tend to promote human happiness, but not only or always our own happiness. They are always useful for *somebody's* interest, but not always for our *own*. We cannot, then, explain our interest in morality and our motivation to act morally just by reference to self-interest.

Hume's third hypothesis, the one he thinks is correct, is that though we are normally motivated by self-interest, self-interest is not our only natural motive. "The interests of society are not, even on their own account, entirely indifferent to us" [43]. We have a natural capacity for sympathy with other human beings, a "natural sentiment of benevolence," and this leads us to take an interest in the well-being of others as well as ourselves. It is this natural benevolence and sympathy, a natural concern for the interests of others and our ability to identify with their interests, that leads us to care about morality and to approve of morally good acts and attitudes.

RECAPITULATION

As I have tried to present Hume's theory, his question from the beginning has been how it is that morality is possible. He has wanted to explain how our ideas of morality arise and, more particularly, how it is that we are motivated to act morally and to take an interest in moral action on the part of others. To answer this question, he needed first to describe what moral actions and motives are like. And after examining both the various kinds of benevolence and the nature of justice, he concludes that morally good acts and traits are those that are *useful*, in the sense that they promote the happiness of someone or other. Since something can be moral in this sense without promoting our own interest, however, the fact that we are self-interested cannot explain our interest in morality. Hume concludes that it is to be explained by reference to a natural sentiment of benevolence and a natural capacity to sympathize with the needs and interest of others.

This explanation for moral motives contrasts sharply with Kant's. While Hume postulates benevolent sentiments as the source of moral motivation, Kant insists that moral motives must derive entirely from reason, independent of sentiment or inclination. Thus, for Kant, moral struggle is conceived as a struggle *between* our rational and our affective natures. For Hume, on the other hand, the demands of morality come from *within* our affective nature. They represent one kind of sentiment or inclination, but one that sometimes conflicts with our self-interested inclinations.

One reason Kant thinks moral motivation must not derive from sentiment is that, in his view, sentiment is too insecure a foundation. Sentiments are too changeable, and so the demands of morality could, if based on sentiment, be too easily escaped. He also seems to think, though, that if morality is based on sentiment, that reduces moral motivation to self-interest. People who take this Kantian attitude may have either of two possible ideas in mind (or they may have some confused combination). One is simply the idea that people do not have motives like benevolence at all. Their only affective motive is self-interest, period. The second idea is that people do sometimes act out of motives like benevolence or kindness but that, even when they do, this *really* just amounts to a form of self-interest.

Hume thinks this Kantian view, in either version, is wrong, and I agree with him. Why it is wrong is worth discussing in some detail since it bears not only on the theoretical question of how we can account for the way people do behave, but also on the practical question of what we can appeal to in justifying the demands of morality to them. Moreover, the idea that everything we do is just self-interested is often put forward with an air of sophisticated cynicism by social theorists in disciplines like economics and political science, where it is thought to vindicate otherwise questionable practices. The assumption of egoism is seen as "hard-nosed" or "realistic," whereas a view like Hume's is thought to rest on soft-headed sentimentality. But Hume was well aware of this alternative to his own view. (Hobbes, writing a century earlier, saw himself as something of a tough-minded realist, while Hume thought he had arguments to refute this alternative.) Rather than focusing directly on Hume's own defense of his position, however, I shall turn to a famous sermon by Joseph Butler, a philosopher and Anglican bishop born some twenty years earlier than Hume. Hume did not know Butler personally, and they disagreed on matters of religion, but Hume admired Butler's philosophical work. Hume repeats the central argument from Butler which I will describe below in Appendix II to the *Enquiry* [92].

BUTLER ON "SELF-LOVE"

I will concentrate here on one work of Butler's and mostly just on the first few pages of it. The few pages I will discuss, however, have had an influence entirely disproportionate to their length on philosophical thinking about egoism and altruism. They are still widely read by philosophers, and they are often thought to contain the classic refutation of the theory that people are motivated solely by self-interest. They come from a sermon titled "Upon the Love of Our Neighbor." This is often referred to as "Sermon Eleven," since it is the eleventh sermon in Butler's *Fifteen Sermons Preached at the Rools Chapel*. (It is actually the fourth in the easily available *Five Sermons*, from which I will quote.)[4]

Butler's sermons are difficult reading, and Sermon Eleven is no exception. Indeed, it is hard to imagine his parishioners staying awake through it, much less following the argument. Butler's aim, in this sermon, is quite simply to "sell" a certain kind of Christian virtue to his flock. He wants to convince men and women that they have a good reason to practice benevolence--"the love of their neighbor." But this task, he thinks, might appear hopeless. For he says in a passage that almost could have been written in the 1990s:

> There is a disposition in men to complain of the viciousness and corruption of the age in which they live as greater than that of former ones; . . . vice and folly takes different turns, and some particular kinds of it are more open and avowed in some ages than in others; and I suppose it may be . . . very much the distinction of the present to profess a contracted spirit and greater regards to self-interest than appears to have been done formerly [46].

In short, Butler says, the "present age" (the early eighteenth century!) is generally thought to be an age of selfishness. The *me*-generation already. And so, he thinks, if he is going to convince people they have a reason to practice Christian benevolence, he will have to show them that benevolence and self-interest are not inconsistent--that benevolence might even be good for them. In Butler's words:

> It seems worth while to inquire whether private interest is likely to be promoted in proportion to the degree in which self-love engrosses us . . . or whether the contracted affection [self-love] may not possibly be so prevalent as to disappoint itself, and even contradict its own end, private good.
> And since, further, there is generally thought to be some peculiar kind of contrariety between self-love and the love of our neighbor . . . it

will be necessary to inquire what respect benevolence hath to self-
love ... [46].

How, then, are self-love (self-interest) and benevolence related? If
it is true that we are self-interested, does that mean that we cannot be
benevolent?   Does rational self-interest automatically rule out
benevolence?   Contrariwise, if we cultivate benevolence, does that
mean that we neglect our self-interest?

These are among the questions Butler means to ask. What he
realizes--and this is something people too frequently fail to realize
when they discuss the question of whether people are motivated only
by self-interest--is that he needs to begin with a *definition* of self-
interest. In his words, he needs "to consider the nature, the object, and
end of . . . self-love" [46].

Surely Butler is right about this. Anyone who thinks, or worries,
that people act only out of self-interest needs to be clear about what
this could mean. In considering whether there is evidence to support
this hypothesis, people need to have a clear idea about what they are
seeking evidence *for*, as well as what would follow from the
hypothesis if it were true. Otherwise, they run the risk of changing
definitions in midstream and so proving or refuting something very
different from what they originally had in mind. Butler's conclusions,
like any conclusion, will hold only relative to his definition. But if his
argument is sound, someone who wants to reject the conclusion has an
obligation to offer, and defend, an alternative definition. How then
does Butler define self-love?

He proceeds by locating self-love among the possible kinds of
human motive and describing its distinctive function. All of us have,
Butler thinks, a large number of specific desires for specific things. He
calls these "particular affections." They include the desire for a swim
or a cold beer on a hot day, the desire to see a movie, to read a book, to
earn more money than one's neighbor, to have one's children do well in
school, or to see hungry children in Ethiopia fed, clothed, and protected
from disease.

Each of these desires, to repeat, is a motive of a kind many people
have. Usually when we do something, we do it *because* we have a
desire to do the kind of thing we do. We go to a movie, for example,
because we want to see a movie, or we buy a hamburger because we are
hungry. But none of these motives is the *same thing* as the motive of
self-love or self-interest. After all, a person could do something out of
self-interest, but not have either of these *particular* motives. So what
is self-love? Butler's answer is that self-love is "a general desire of
[one's] own happiness." This desire is different from any "particular
affection." Particular affections each have as their objects "this or

that particular external thing," like a swim, a movie, or success for one's children. The object of self-love, on the other hand, is "somewhat internal--our own happiness, enjoyment, satisfaction; whether we have or have not a distinct particular perception what it is or wherein it consists" [47]. When we act out of self-love, when that is our motive, we are acting out of a desire for happiness or pleasure. This is a different desire from any particular affection, and any particular affection is different from it.

This latter point needs to be stressed. It is crucial for understanding Butler. It is true, of course, that every particular affection I have is one of *my* particular affections. I like golf, and you may not, so we may not even have the same kinds of desire; but even if we both like golf, my desire to play is mine, and yours is yours. If I act on mine, I am the one that satisfies my desire, not you. Still, the fact that it is my desire does not mean that it is the same as my desire for my happiness. Both desires are mine, but they are not the same desire. They are no more the same than my desire to play golf is the same desire as my desire to finish writing this book. In fact, the two conflict right now. Moreover, since finishing the book will make me happier (overall!) than playing golf this afternoon, the desire to play golf conflicts with my desire to be happy. But both are still my desires.

Different people, of course, have different particular affections; and, indeed, nonhuman creatures have particular affections as well. Self-love, on the other hand, Butler sees as a desire peculiar to creatures like us. It stems from our nature as "sensible creatures who can reflect upon themselves and their own interest or happiness, so as to have that interest an object to their minds" [47].

As Butler defines self-love, then, we act out of self-love when we aim not merely at the object of some desire--like an ice cream cone--but at happiness, satisfaction, or enjoyment as well. Sometimes we have no thought of pleasure or happiness at all. We just want the ice cream. Acting from self-love typically involves some self-conscious calculation. We don't just follow our immediate inclination for something, but we stop to think about which of our various inclinations might be most satisfying. In fact, though Butler doesn't explicitly say this, a good sign that our action is motivated by self-interest might be that we do something (like eating healthy but tasteless food) for which we have no particular desire. This is just the kind of thing we do when we are focusing on something like our overall well-being or happiness but not on the object of immediate inclination.

Butler's definition of self-love, or self-interest, is to my mind both plausible and helpful. I know of no better definition. But it has, as Butler points out, a most interesting consequence: *It is impossible for anyone to act, successfully,* only *out of self-interest.* Why? To act out of self-interest is to seek enjoyment or satisfaction, but enjoyment or satisfaction derives from doing something one likes for its own sake, something for which, in Butler's language, one has a particular affection. The particular affection itself must be aimed at a particular object--like a piece of pizza--and not at the pleasure arising from the pizza, since there would be no satisfaction from the pizza without a prior desire *for it* [47]. And if one is not acting partly on some particular desire, there is no possibility of achieving any satisfaction at all.

The same point could be made a different way. Suppose someone actually had only one desire, namely, the desire Butler calls "self-love." What are we to imagine this person doing? She wants happiness, but that, by itself, gives no guidance at all. She can't go to the supermarket and fill up her cart with boxes of happiness. In fact, she has nothing at all to do unless she acquires at least one further interest, like an interest in tennis, or in reading. In that case, if she wants to be happy, she can do something about it, namely, play tennis. But that works only because she has an independent liking for tennis.

Nothing I have said, and nothing Butler says, is meant to deny that people often act out of self-love. They do, and Butler thinks they do. They often take a certain course of action because they want to be happier or to enjoy themselves. But they cannot do this at all unless they have specific desires in addition to the desire for happiness. When people act successfully out of self-interest, they are motivated also partly by some specific desire. But then these specific desires have, as it were, a life of their own. They give us an interest in doing this or that whether or not, in the specific circumstances, it is actually the best thing to do in terms of cool, calculating self-love. And when some specific desire--some "particular affection"--moves us to act directly, then it is that desire that moves us, not self-love. This is true whether the desire is love of our children or a desire for a cold beer.

Butler's original question, we should recall, was whether people motivated largely by self-love could be given a good reason--a reason that appealed to their self-love--to practice Christian benevolence and to cultivate Christian love for their neighbors. His answer should now be clear. First, there is no essential conflict between self-love and benevolence, any more than there is a conflict between self-love and love of beer [51]. Both love of beer and love of humankind are particular affections. Each one is a possible way of achieving satisfaction, and so each is something that a person motivated by self-interest might well want to cultivate and act on. But the argument goes further than this. Along with "nice" motives like kindness, along with neutral ones like love of beer, men and women also have "particular affections" like greed, cruelty, and envy. How do these relate to self-love?

In part, the answer is the same for all particular affections. Each, if acted on, is a potential source of some satisfaction. However, as Butler is quick to point out, some are easier to satisfy, and are more likely to lead to long-term happiness, than others. Envy and greed, after all, are like a treadmill. They are never fully satisfied, and they disrupt personal relationships. Here is where Butler thinks benevolent motives have a real edge. Not only are they easily satisfied, but they lead to easier relations with others. So, Butler thinks, to the extent that we have control over our particular affections, we do well, from the point of view of our own happiness, to cultivate something like the Christian virtues.

There is a further point here, related to what has sometimes been called the "paradox of hedonism." As Butler observes, an obsessive concern with our own well-being is likely to *prevent* us from being happy: "*Disengagement* is absolutely necessary to enjoyment; and a person may have so steady and fixed an eye upon his own interest, . . . as may hinder him from *attending* to many gratifications within his reach . . ." [48-49]. So again, it may well be that we do best for ourselves if we cultivate a disinterested concern and affection for others. Having done so, however, when we act out of this concern, we are never acting *merely* out of self-interest. We are acting out of benevolence, and that is a distinct, additional motive.

If Butler is right here, and if he is also right that morality involves something like kindness or benevolence, then his "Sermon Eleven" answers the question about morality: "What's in it for me?" And, if we understand the question "why be moral?" as this question, it answers that question, too. But there is a good further point as well. By emphasizing the number and variety of the motives people normally have--by showing what a mistake it is to reduce all these to a single motive of self-interest--Butler also shows that it is possible for people to take an interest in moral requirements and to be moved to act on them even if this doesn't, directly or indirectly, promote their own happiness.

BUTLER'S SIGNIFICANCE

Perhaps the single most important thing to get from Butler is an appreciation for the huge variety of human motives and desires, both good and bad, exciting and mundane. Self-interest is a constant among people. Everyone has it to some extent. But what makes us the distinct men and women we are is not self-interest, but rather the specific collection of particular affections that make up "that particular nature" according to which a person is made [47]. What is *interesting* about a person is not that he or she sometimes acts from self-interest--everyone does that--but rather what particular desires he or she seeks to satisfy when pursuing this goal. That is what tells us whether we want that person for a friend or a colleague, or whether to invite him or her to a party. And that is certainly what is relevant to moral evaluation. Good people have the right particular desires and bad people the wrong ones.

What I have just said should sound familiar. It is very much like what Aristotle says. What people have when they have the virtues is, roughly, the right desires. They have, in Butler's terms, *particular affections* for truth, and justice, and for the right amount of things like sensual pleasures. And Aristotle would also appreciate Butler's point that it is not possible to seek only pleasure and actually succeed in getting it. Aristotle, like Butler, sees pleasure or enjoyment as something that we get only when we take a direct interest in some activity, or engaging in it for its own sake and doing it (at least partly) because we find it intrinsically interesting. To the extent that we are preoccupied with "the bottom line," with happiness or pleasure themselves, we are likely to miss the very thing we most want.

Kant, on the other hand, may have been seriously confused on a number of these points. At least I suspect that confusion about the relation between self-interest and particular affections (i.e., direct inclinations) helps to explain his insistence that the morally best action is based on reason alone, not on any inclination. Accepting the idea--which Butler also accepts--that satisfying any inclination can give rise to pleasure, he may infer that any inclination is a desire for nothing but pleasure. That, we have seen, is a fallacious inference. But if Kant made it, it would lead him to conclude that each desire is equivalent to self-love, and so (assuming that self-love and a good will can't be the same) that acting with a good will can't be acting on an inclination. That specific inclinations must be different from self-love, however, is precisely the point of Butler's most famous passage: "That all particular appetites and passions are toward *external things themselves,* distinct from the *pleasure arising from them,* is manifested from hence--that there could not be this pleasure were it not for that prior suitableness between the object and the passion" [47].

Kant is by no means the only philosopher who tends to reduce all desires to self-interest. There is evidence that Hobbes, Bentham, and Mill all made the same assumption. Even Butler concedes that we *could* define self-interest to mean the same thing as "acting on one of our own desires." But he points out that that would make it totally uninteresting to say that anyone acts from self-interest. The interesting question would remain the question Butler always thinks most interesting anyway, namely, what particular desires does the person have? For, even though we all act out of desires, our particular desires are very different [47-48].

Hume does not fall into the trap of thinking that people's motives are all somehow reducible to self-interest. He is well aware of their diversity and is impressed by it. And Butler's arguments show that there is no need for Hume to retreat from his belief that there are motives other than self-interest. It is fully possible that people are motivated by benevolence just as much as Hume thinks; and so there is no general philosophical problem with Hume's attempt to explain our interest in morality in terms of the assumption that we are to some extent benevolent.

Butler's aim is to justify morality--to justify it *to* people in terms of their presumed self-love--and he clearly assumes that benevolence, a direct concern for the well-being of others, is at least a major part of what morality requires. In this respect, too, Hume is like Butler. Hume thinks morally good acts or character traits are those that have "utility," in the sense that they tend to promote human happiness or well-being. More generally, he thinks that when we view our decisions from the moral point of view, when we evaluate others from the moral point of view, we "depart from [our] private and particular situation, and . . . chuse a point of view common . . . with others" [Hume, 75]. And this point of view is something like a generalized benevolence. When we take up the moral point of view, we take a general interest in the well-being of all, and we judge our own acts as well as those of others in terms of their tendency to promote human interests generally. Hume explains our ability to take up this point of view in terms of our natural capacity for sympathy and our natural benevolence.

One question about Hume's theory is whether he is naive in thinking that people are or even could be motivated by something like benevolence. This was the question that led me to discuss Butler. But, before turning to Butler, I raised another question about Hume's theory that is independent of this one about the possibility of benevolent motives. The second question had to do with Hume's theory of justice, and to that second question I must now return.

The problem is this: While Hume's general opinion is that morally good acts are those that tend to promote happiness, he also thinks that justice is a moral requirement. But, as I observed earlier, Hume agrees that individual acts of justice do not necessarily promote happiness. How is justice related to the good of individuals and society, and even if we are naturally concerned with the good of others and the good of society, is that the *kind* of concern that could explain an interest in justice?

This is a crucial issue for this chapter, and for the whole book. Indeed, it is a crucial issue for moral philosophy generally. Perhaps we agree with Hume and other modern philosophers that a part of morality is concerned with human well-being in general, not just with one's own good. If we do agree, then the arguments of Hume and Butler establish that most people also have good reasons to act morally; for people certainly can, and most do, have a certain amount of natural benevolence. But, whether we think of morality as concerned with one's own good, or with the good of people generally, it remains a puzzle how the requirements of justice fit into the picture. First, they do not directly and in every case have good consequences either for the agent or for other people. Hence, why we should think of them as moral at all is puzzling. Second, if we are concerned about how a person could have a reason or motive to act as justice requires, we again have a puzzle. Not only does self-interest not directly lead to just action, but neither does kindness or benevolence. If there is good reason to be suspicious about the rationality of morality, it probably applies most to the requirements of justice.

HOBBES ON THE NEED FOR SOCIAL RULES
AND THE REASON FOR OBEYING THEM

A century earlier than Hume, Thomas Hobbes confronted a question very similar to the question I have just raised about Hume's work. An English philosopher and an empiricist like Hume, Hobbes wrote influentially on a wide range of subjects. It is often said that the turmoil of the English revolution of the seventeenth century influenced his political philosophy.

Like Hume, Hobbes believes it is essential, if people are to live decent lives at all, that their interactions be regulated by social rules. Most especially, he thinks it essential that people live up to their agreements with one another. Indeed, the requirement "that men perform their covenants made" [119][5] is, for Hobbes, the essence of the requirement of justice. (For Hume, justice involves both keeping promises and respecting property.) In addition, Hobbes thinks it essential that people reciprocate the trust and good will of others [125], that they accommodate themselves to one another [125-126], and that they submit their disputes to impartial mediators [129]. Most generally, he thinks that people must submit to the governance of a single authoritative individual or body of individuals and follow the laws or rules this "sovereign" lays down. Of all the agreements people must keep, this agreement to be ruled by a sovereign government is the most important in Hobbes's theory.

In order to make vivid the importance of obedience to political authority and compliance with established rules, Hobbes makes use of the idea of a *state of nature*. He imagines what it would be like for people to live without mutually acceptable rules and without any commonly acknowledged political authority. He concludes, in a famous passage, that in this state of nature there would be "no place for industry, because the fruit thereof is uncertain: and consequently no culture of the earth; no navigation nor use of the commodities that may be imported by sea; . . . no knowledge . . . no account of time; no arts; no letters; no society; and, which is worst of all, continual fear and danger of violent death; and the life of man solitary, poor, nasty, brutish and short" [107].

In these passages, Hobbes is making the same point about the usefulness of social rules and practices that Hume makes, but he is doing it negatively: While Hume stresses the *advantages* of rules of justice and argues that these rules exist only when they benefit everyone, Hobbes emphasizes the *disadvantages* of a general *failure* to comply with such rules. Clearly, though, both agree with the idea that we are all better off if we all adhere to systems of social rules and respect established systems of authority than any of us would be if no one did.

There is another interesting point of similarity between Hobbes and Hume. While both think it desirable, from the viewpoint of individual members of society, that people accept and comply with social rules, neither sets out anything like a full list of specific rules. Neither claims that only one system of rules is the best or correct one. Justice or morality requires that we follow some rules, that we make an accommodation with one another; but what those rules are or should be is not something set down in the abstract. Except for the very general idea, in Hume, that rules of justice are beneficial, and the general idea in Hobbes that one ought to keep covenants, specifically the covenant to obey rules laid down by a sovereign authority, exactly what we are required to do depends on our specific circumstances.

Hobbes and Hume differ, however, in their ideas about just what these circumstances are. In the case of Hobbes, what we are required to do depends mainly on what the political sovereign lays down as law. According to Hume, on the other hand, rules of justice depend on conventions that arise in a natural way out of the interactions of individuals mainly pursuing their own interest. This is one of Hume's most ingenious ideas; yet if Hobbes is right, Hume's conventions would be impossible! I need to explain why. It will take some time.

Hume thinks rules of justice, such as property rules, are beneficial for everyone. It is not hard to see how this could be true. Suppose no such rules were recognized and obeyed. In that case, it would hardly be worthwhile for anyone, say, to till a field and plant a crop. Anyone who did would have to expect that others would "harvest" the crop for themselves as soon as it was ripe. So why make the effort? On the other hand, if men and women came to have a common idea about which fields belonged to whom, and if they respected those boundaries, then they could plant crops in their own fields confident that they could reap the benefits. Indeed, if property rights were respected, not everyone would have to grow crops. Those who wanted to could plant many acres, while others established mills, raised sheep, or manufactured cloth. The latter could then trade their cloth for the food raised by others. In short, society would begin to benefit from specialization and the division of labor. But, again, it is essential that there be a widely recognized and respected system of property rules in the background. Otherwise, it wouldn't pay for the farmer to plant many acres, and it would be too risky for the cloth manufacturer to leave the farm on the assumption that there would be food to purchase. In general, then, there is some reason to think that everyone will be better off in the situation in which everyone respects property rights than anyone would be if no one did.

Hume accepts this kind of reasoning, and he thinks that since everyone would benefit from established systems of property, contract, and the like, we should expect that people would work them out and come to accept them naturally. He imagines a natural development of the kind anthropologists sometimes speculate must have taken place. People are brought together by sexual attraction, a family forms, and "particular rules being found requisite for its subsistence, these are immediately embraced. . . ." And, if other families join them, the rules are extended to include these new families [26]. But just how do the rules develop? Hume insists that no one consciously invents them, and they don't come to be established by people promising to obey them. Indeed, the idea of promising or agreeing is something that *itself* has to be invented. Instead, Hume says that people settle on rules by a process that he calls "convention." Rules of justice, he thinks, are analogous to conventions of language (rules about which words mean what) and conventions about money (how much different beads, shells, or trinkets are worth). Such ideas come to be accepted gradually and naturally. It is like the process, he says, in which two people rowing a boat, each with one oar, would gradually coordinate their rhythm so that they go in a straight line, even if they couldn't communicate by speech [95]. For another example, we might imagine rules of the road. Suppose, at first, that there is no "official" rule about which side of the road to drive on. Still, people would want to avoid head-on collisions, so each would try to see which side most others were driving on. If most drove on the left, say, each newcomer would have a good reason to do the same. And the more this happened, the stronger the reason for each to go along. Soon, the situation would stabilize with practically everyone driving on the same side.

As Hume sees it, rules of justice will develop in just this way. As families form and are joined by other families to form societies, people will fall into accepting the same ideas about what belongs to whom, about how new property can be acquired or transferred, and so on. Just as each wants to follow the prevailing ideas about which side of the road to drive on, people will also want to follow the prevailing conventions of property. In each case, self-interest will lead them to do so, and as they come to see how everyone benefits from rules of property, benevolence will lead them to view rules of property as morally desirable as well.

Hume's idea is striking in its clarity and simplicity. It allows Hume to explain how it is that the rules governing property and contract in different societies are often different and, at the same time, how people come to feel committed to the rules of their own society and come to view them as moral requirements. Moreover, it allows him to explain the motives we have for being just (for respecting rights like property rights) without postulating any *special* moral sense, any built-in special motives for being just over and above basic self-interest and benevolence. However, it is hard to reconcile Hume's ideas about the origin and development of moral ideas and his explanation for moral behavior with Hobbes's insights.

Recall Hobbes's picture of what the state of nature--society without any established sovereign government--would be like. According to Hobbes, human life would be "solitary, poor, nasty, brutish and short" [107]. But Hume seems clearly to assume the opposite. In his view, people would come to share ideas about rules of various kinds, would see the advantages of obedience both for themselves and others, and, impelled both by natural self-interest and benevolence, would follow these rules. Hobbes agrees that people need rules and that they benefit from general obedience to rules of the kind Hume described. But he denies that they will adopt them and obey them in the absence of a coercive government that enforces them with threats of punishment. For that reason, he thinks that the most basic requirement of morality (the second law of nature) is that people agree with one another to give up their natural freedom and to accept a common government as sovereign. Moreover, justice (the third law of nature) demands that they keep their "covenants" with one another, including, of course, the basic agreement to establish a sovereign government in the first place [110, 119]. But even these requirements, Hobbes thinks, are requirements people will have no reason to follow until a sovereign is established to enforce it.

Clearly, Hobbes and Hume disagree about the possibility of stable social cooperation in the absence of a coercive government. What is the basis for their disagreement and how might it be resolved? One possible suggestion is that they disagree because they have very different ideas about what people are naturally like--what motives people naturally have. Hobbes, it might be thought, sees people as being motivated solely by self-interest and greed, while Hume claims that people have a naturally benevolent side to their nature. According to this interpretation, Hume is more optimistic about human nature than is Hobbes, and that explains why he thinks people will naturally adopt and comply with useful social rules like rules of property and contract. Hobbes sees people as basically bad, and that is why he thinks we cannot function decently at all without a powerful, coercive government.

What I have just described is a commonly held idea about what leads Hobbes to his conclusions. People who accept this idea go on to suggest that if we give up Hobbes's pessimistic assumptions about human nature, we can also avoid his conclusions about the need for a powerful, coercive government. But I believe this account of the issue between Hobbes and Hume is mistaken, for at least two reasons. First, though Hume believes that benevolent attitudes *help* to guarantee compliance with rules of justice, he thinks self-interest alone is enough to lead people to adopt and follow such rules. Second, there are problems about the *structure* of beneficial social rules, problems which Hobbes apparently appreciated, that may lead even *benevolent* people to disobey them. Let me illustrate this problem with an example.

Where I live, there is a public television station. It is largely supported by voluntary donations from the community. However, as in other communities, only a small proportion of the residents actually make contributions. Why? It is not that people don't watch the station. True, public TV is often not as entertaining as *Cheers*, but plenty of people still watch the public TV news and business reports, and their children watch *Sesame Street* and *Mr. Rogers*. Many more people enjoy and benefit from the programs than actually pay. So why don't they contribute? The reason, it seems likely, is that each sees that his or her individual contribution is not *necessary* to keep the programs coming. It is unlike going to the movie theater. There, if you don't pay, you can't watch. But with public TV, each individual can still watch, even without paying. Indeed, and this is the interesting point in light of Hume's assumption that people are benevolent, even if individuals care both about their own interests and about the interests of others who watch public TV, that *still* doesn't give them a conclusive reason to contribute. The reason is the same. *For each individual person, public TV will still go on, regardless of whether that person contributes.*

What Hobbes realized is that many of the rules that benefit society are a lot like a rule in our era that viewers of public TV ought to contribute. In many cases, a particular individual can disobey them, while still benefiting from the cooperation of others, and without diminishing their benefits either. That is why he thought life in "the state of nature" would be so bad. People might see the advantages of having some agreed-upon rules of conduct and of respecting those rules in their dealings with one another. But they would also see that, as individuals, they could disobey the rules in particular cases while still benefiting from the cooperation of others. Moreover, each would be aware that the others would see the same possibility. Each would worry that the others would start cheating, that the whole system would break down, and that cooperation on his or her part would just be wasted. So, not because they are particularly bad or greedy, but just because they have a rational understanding of the situation they face, they would concentrate not on productive work but on self-protection. The state of nature, as Hobbes says, would tend to turn into a state of war--a "war of every man against every man" [Ch. 13, 108]. In the absence of a coercive government to enforce rules by threatening penalties for disobedience, relations among persons would be something like relations among sovereign nations. Just think of the arms race.

Several important points about this discussion need to be kept in mind. First, the problem that Hobbes emphasizes--the problem that individuals may often be tempted to violate important social rules in particular cases--does not really depend on an assumption that people are motivated just by self-interest. Even people who are concerned about the welfare of others will not always follow such rules. Think about your own case. I, for example, do contribute to public TV, but I don't give nearly as much as I might; and there are many similar causes from which I benefit but to which I give nothing. But it is not just narrow self-interest that limits my contributions. Money contributed to public TV is money I don't spend on my children's education or on parties or gifts for my family and friends. If I were moved purely by a benevolent concern to help others, I could do more direct good by writing a check directly to the local campaign to feed the homeless than by sending it to public TV.

Second, Hume himself, though he tries to explain our commitment to justice in terms of benevolence and self-interest, actually recognizes this problem. In a number of passages, as I have already noted, he observes that strict compliance with rules of justice will sometimes do more harm, or at least less good, than noncompliance. Of course, property rules are not just like requirements that we support public TV. Often, perhaps usually, stealing does direct harm to the victim, and so benevolent people will resist it, even when it would benefit them. But that isn't always so. People will sometimes rationalize "a little shoplifting" by saying that no one will notice and no one will be harmed. And the trouble is, sometimes that is true. I suspect the local supermarket will throw away some of the oranges in its bin. They are already paid for, and they will go bad before they are sold. If I take one, I am better off, and no one is worse off.

Finally, nothing I have said is meant to deny that social rules, like rules of property, really are good for people, both individually and collectively. It is just that their *connection* to individual good is not always direct. What seems to be true is something like this: If everyone respects rules like rules of property, then everyone is better off than if no one does. That is why, when we argue with someone who tries to defend, for example, shoplifting or cheating on an exam, the natural response is "what if everyone did that?" When we compare the two extreme cases--universal cooperation and universal noncooperation--cooperation wins. If everyone shoplifts, the social costs are staggering. But, as every clever person can say in reply to "what if everyone . . .": "*I'm* not *everyone.*" So, even though we all depend on the fact that most people do cooperate, it does not follow that each of us, individually, has a motive to do so.

In the last few pages I have been siding mainly with Hobbes. I have agreed with him that, especially in a large society, benevolence and rational self-interest are not enough to guarantee stable social cooperation, even when general cooperation is, in a straightforward sense, beneficial for everyone. Given this point, Hume may seem naive; for it is a mistake to *infer* from the fact that everyone benefits from universal cooperation that my own, individual cooperation is necessary or even desirable. To be fair to Hume, though, he does at a number of points [e.g., 81-82, 93-94] make it clear that he recognizes this problem. Moreover, he even, like Hobbes, indicates that government has a role to play in motivating us to cooperate [34]. And there are certainly some things to be said in defense of Hume's relative optimism.

Clever people will recognize that they, as individuals, can cheat in particular cases without jeopardizing the whole system of cooperation on which they rely. However, they will not want to advertise this fact. They won't want to encourage others to cheat, and they won't want others to think they can't be trusted. Others, after all, won't be indifferent to the way they act. Whenever there is any danger of detection, therefore, individuals will have an incentive, based on nothing but rational self-interest, to comply with rules and respect rights. Hume actually mentions this consideration [77], and it is one that Hobbes also should have considered. Indeed, if we focus on Hobbes, there are some serious problems within *his* theory, too. His general idea is that, given the nature of social cooperation, individuals will never have sufficient motive to cooperate unless there is a powerful government that can provide an artificial motive in the form of threatened punishment. But now suppose we ask how this government of Hobbes is supposed to work. There will have to be a police force, and the police officers will have to be relied upon to come to work in the morning and not to spend their whole day taking coffee breaks. What will keep them working? And if the answer is that their superiors will watch them, what is to keep *the superiors* in line?

Of course--and this tends to support Hobbes's pessimism--we do have problems with both public employees and employees in the private sector loafing on the job. On the other hand, if things were as bad as Hobbes seems to think, it is hard to see how even the government that he sees as so essential could get off the ground. Surely the truth is that most people have sufficient built-in motives to comply with beneficial rules most of the time. But just as surely, *Hobbes* is right in thinking that the threat of punishment is a useful, and sometimes necessary, additional motive. Indeed, as I have noted, even if Hume is right and most people have "internal" motives to comply with rules and respect rights, the existence of external sanctions gives them some assurance that others will cooperate as well and that their efforts won't be wasted. In any case, none of this settles the question of whether Hume is right about exactly which motives we have and exactly which motives best explain the fact that we manage, most of the time, to do what he thinks morality requires.

TWO PARTS OF MORALITY

For the Greek theorists, the point of moral virtues and moral attitudes, ultimately, was to contribute to the well-being of their possessors. For modern theorists, on the other hand, morality has a different point. It serves to secure or protect the interests of others, to promote their well-being, or to make possible the benefits of social cooperation. It appears to us as a demand that we be kind or compassionate, or it appears as a matter of duty or obligation. All this is generally agreed, though theorists differ as to just what it requires and how our interest in morality is to be explained. But leaving aside the Greek conception of morality and focusing on the modern idea of morality as involving mostly a concern with social good and the good of others, we can still distinguish two quite different parts of morality.

On the one hand, morality is concerned directly with the well-being of other individuals or groups. The moral person is the person who is kind, who tries not to harm others or even to hurt someone's feelings. Moral men and women are concerned with the plight of the homeless and with victims of natural disasters and social disintegration, wherever they occur. They contribute to the Red Cross or CARE, and they support legislation to increase humanitarian foreign aid. But this represents only one part of morality. Morality also requires that we respect people's rights and comply with social rules, that we do our fair share in community projects, that we treat people fairly, and that we keep our word. These latter requirements, of course, include the requirements Hume thought of as matters of justice.

It was one of Hume's contributions to moral philosophy that he recognized the differences between these two kinds of moral requirement. Another of his contributions was his idea that it might be possible to understand morality by understanding the role it plays in our lives as individuals and as members of society. He hoped he could explain how people come to be interested in morality, why they think it important, and how they are motivated to do what it requires in terms of ordinary, everyday ideas about what people care about and what they need. This is very different from the idea of Kant that none of our ordinary inclinations could explain moral behavior. It is very different from his idea that we can explain motives to act morally only as motives of reason. But, in spite of Hume's insights into the differences between requirements of justice and requirements of benevolence, it seems clear that he underestimated the extent of these differences. In particular, while it is plausible that he can explain the motivation to promote or protect the well-being of others in terms of a natural motive of benevolence, it seems implausible that motives like benevolence or self-interest can adequately explain our motives to respect justice.

I wish to pursue this point further in this section by explaining a rather technical problem that has received a lot of attention in recent years from philosophers, economists, and decision theorists. It is called "the prisoners' dilemma." It gets its name from this story: Hank and Butch have been arrested on suspicion of bank robbery. The DA knows they did it, but he doesn't have adequate evidence. He slaps them in separate cells, and he goes to each with the following proposal: "If you turn state's evidence and confess, I'll let you off with probation and throw the book at the other guy. (And if he confesses but you don't, I'll throw the book at *you*.) But if neither of you confesses, I will give you the maximum possible sentence for a concealed weapons charge, and that will be worse than probation for bank robbery." What should Hank and Butch do? Both prefer probation to doing any jail time, and both prefer a short sentence for the weapons charge to a long sentence for bank robbery. Yet both fear that the other will confess, to try to get probation, and both know that, if both confess, the DA will no longer need to keep the bargain and can send them both up for bank robbery.

A complicated story, but it can be illustrated with a simple game. The game is played by two players, Al and Mary. Each is placed in a separate room, and each has two buttons to push, one red and one green. When the clock strikes twelve, each is to push a button. If both push green, each gets $10. If both push red, each gets $0. If Al pushes red but Mary pushes green, Al gets $20 and Mary loses $10. Finally, if Mary pushes red and Al green, then Mary gets the $20 but Al loses the $10. These rules can be summarized in the following table.

MARY

		Green	Red
	Green	$10, $10	-$10, $20
AL			
	Red	$20, -$10	$0, $0

The dollar figures in each cell of this table represent the payoffs to each player. The first figure is the payoff to Al, the second the payoff to Mary. Thus, as one can see, how much each gets depends partly on what he or she does, partly on what the other person does. In that respect, this is like any competitive game. (In tennis, for example, I may do well to hit a drop shot, but only if my opponent does not anticipate it.)

Let us assume that each player wants only to have as much money as possible. What should each do? Consider Al. He might push green, if he thought Mary would do so--but if he were sure she would push green, he would be better off pushing red. After all, 20 is more than 10. But that means pushing green is risky for her, so she might think of pushing red (and Al is smart enough to see that she might). So suppose she pushes red. If Al knows this, then again, Al does better to push red too, since 0 is better than -10. In short, red is better for Al than green, no matter what Mary does. So, he should push red. But, notice, the strategic situation is exactly the same for Mary, so, Mary should also push red. If each is rational in the pursuit of his or her self-interest, each will end up with $0. But this seems paradoxical, for if both had chosen what is not rational, namely, green, then each would have $10.

Whether or not this result is paradoxical, it is at least clear that this kind of game presents each player with a dilemma--but it is a dilemma that is very common in real life. It is exactly the dilemma that faces sellers in a competitive market. (If both sell their groceries for an extra-high price, then each will make a big profit. But if one does so, the other will be able to get all the customers by selling at a lower price. Each sees this, so each sells at a low price to begin with, and each makes just enough to stay in business and feed the family.)

A solution, it might appear, would be an agreement to cooperate. (Let's both push green, or let's both sell lettuce for $4 per head.) Of course, in the case of grocers, society makes this agreement illegal. It is called "conspiracy in restraint of trade." We *want* grocers to be caught in this kind of dilemma, because we want the lowest possible price. But even if people do try to make such cooperative arrangements, they tend to be unstable. For suppose Al and Mary agree to push green. If Al thinks Mary will keep her agreement, then he can make a quick 20 bucks by pushing red! And the same goes for Mary. This point brings us back to the problems of justice and social cooperation that Hume and Hobbes raised.

Both Hobbes and Hume think of rules of justice as a kind of cooperative arrangement or cooperative scheme. For each, what justice requires of individuals is that they comply with such rules--that they act as if they have made a commitment to a cooperative arrangement and that they keep this commitment. They both see this kind of social cooperation as being beneficial for everyone, but Hobbes, more than Hume, also sees that social cooperation is intrinsically unstable. Hobbes's key insight, indeed, is that social arrangements are often unstable in just the way that a cooperative solution to the prisoners' dilemma is unstable. The analogy isn't perfect, but it is close. We are all better off if we all respect property rules than if none of us do; but if all the *others* respect such rules, any one of us can benefit from social peace and prosperity while still not complying.

Both in the case of the prisoners' dilemma and in the case of social rules, the problem stems from the fact that the benefits of cooperation are partly independent of one's own actions. In the case of Al and Mary, the outcome for Al depends partly on what Mary does. Al can benefit from Mary's pushing green, even if he pushes red. Indeed, he gets even more. Moreover, he can't assure himself of even $10 by pushing green himself, for *she* might push red. The same is true for property rules, for paying taxes, for maintaining the smog control devices in one's car, and many other kinds of cooperation. We value the benefits of successful cooperation, but we can get many of these benefits even if we ourselves don't cooperate; and we can't guarantee them by cooperating. Yet, just as we think it morally desirable to treat other particular people with kindness and to refrain from harming them, we also think it morally important to cooperate in situations like these. What I hope is that we are now in a position to see just how very different these two kinds of moral requirement are.

The requirement that we treat people kindly tells us to do particular acts that are themselves kind in the sense that their immediate consequence is some benefit or relief for someone. It is obvious that men and women who have kind and benevolent desires will be moved to do kind acts. The existence of such desires will explain our interest in this part of morality as Hume wants to do. People who have these desires will have a reason to do as this part of morality requires. For them, and for this part of morality, there will be a clear answer to the question "why be moral?"

The acts required by justice, as Hume understands it, may not themselves have direct good consequences, either for the agent or for anyone else. Things like stability, security, and predictability, which derive from rules of property and contract, are in Hume's words "the result of . . . the whole system of actions"[94], just as, in the game with Al and Mary, if Al ends up with $10 it will be not just because of something he did, but because of what he *and* Mary did. (He might have done the same thing and lost $10, had Mary acted differently!) What this means is that motives like kindness and benevolence or, for that matter, self-interest cannot easily explain why people do what justice requires. These motives are directed toward consequences, but the consequences of just actions are (often) independent of anything we ourselves do. This means not only that Hume cannot invoke these motives to explain our interest in justice but also that we cannot reasonably appeal to these motives in answer to the question "why be moral?" when what is at stake is requirements of justice.

Now, having pointed out some of the differences between these two parts of morality, it will be useful to see how they appear in some of the other theories we have examined in earlier chapters. Consider the case of Aristotle. He assumes that people have, as one of their basic concerns, something very much like what Butler calls "self-love"--a general desire for a happy and satisfying life. And, like Butler, he thinks that the quality of one's life depends on what "particular affections" one acquires. Specifically, Aristotle thinks one benefits by acquiring the moral virtues; but these virtues are not reducible to any single kind of concern. They are a motley lot. They include things like generosity, a part of what Hume would include under "benevolence." They also include truthfulness and justice and, of course, they include things like courage, temperance, and even wittiness. It seems to be an important part of Aristotle's idea that, though many of these virtues consist (in part) of specific desires, the desires involved in different virtues are different. What generous persons want is to share some part of what they have with others or with the community. What just people want is not to take what they don't deserve or aren't entitled to and to see to it that the deserts and rights of others are respected. And so on.

The differences between Hume's and Aristotle's approaches should be quite striking. While Hume tries to find a single common element in moral motivation, a single kind of motive--disinterested benevolence-- that underlies our interest in morality, Aristotle emphasizes the diversity of moral motives that make up the virtues. As a result, the problem I have raised for Hume's theory of morality, the problem that he seems to recognize two very different kinds of moral requirement, would be no problem for Aristotle. For a person who has been brought up to have the desires characteristic of the virtue of justice, it is easy to explain the motive to act justly, to do his or her share, and so forth. For having the virtue of justice just is having desires to do these things. And, for that person, there is an answer to the question "why be moral?"

Of course, much of modern moral philosophy has been haunted by the thought that people can only act selfishly, and so maybe no one really has desires like a desire to respect the rights of others. But as we have seen, Hume and Butler have decisive arguments against this idea, so it is certainly not impossible to offer the kind of explanation for moral behavior that Aristotle offers. Indeed, having given up the idea that people have only selfish motives, Hume might have gone further in recognizing the diversity of possible particular motives. Along with a benevolent desire to promote the good of others, he might also have postulated a motive to cooperate, to do one's part, or some such, and that would go a long way toward explaining the fact that people respect rules of justice as well as act kindly toward others. Still, even though people have, and are capable of acquiring, a great variety of concerns and motives, that does not mean that self-interest is not among these concerns, and so, for many, "why be moral?" will mean, at least in part, "what's in it for me?" The answer, with regard to particular acts--especially the acts required by justice--will often be "nothing." But that, as Aristotle and Butler would certainly grant, does not mean that people would not be better off, in the long run, having acquired a desire to cooperate with others. But Hume and Hobbes would insist that whether it is good for me to have such a desire will depend, in part, on the kind of world I live in and, specifically, on whether others around me are cooperative as well.

If Hume overemphasizes the motive of promoting good consequences in explaining moral behavior, it might be argued that Kant errs in going to the other extreme. It is significant, however, that one of the basic ideas in Kant's theory, namely, the idea that one ought to do only what one can will that everyone do, or only what accords with laws that everyone would legislate for everyone to follow, seems to be a lot like the ideas, in Hume and Hobbes, that people need to follow rules of justice. For Hume and Hobbes both see these requirements as requirements that must be followed by people generally, since people are much better off as a whole just when these rules are generally followed. It is as if Kant saw clearly how a concern for good consequences would fail to produce just action in those cases in which the consequences are independent of a person's own specific choices. That may be one reason why he thought we could explain moral action only if there is a direct motive just to obey the moral law for its own sake. At least one part of morality requires compliance with rules and respect for conventionally established systems of rights and authority, as if compliance is something good in itself. What Hume and Hobbes recognized, on the other hand, was the extent to which these requirements depend on local conventions and on the enactments of locally established authorities. From their point of view, the response to Kant's idea that we must follow the moral law is "*which* law?" And we have seen in the preceding chapter that we can get conflicting results when we apply Kant's Universalization Principle to a moral problem. What seems to be needed is an account of how conventional rules can come to have the force of something like Kantian moral laws and how they can *reasonably* be seen as having this force. This is an issue to which we will have to return in the last chapter.

MORAL CONTROVERSY AND THE
TWO PARTS OF MORALITY

In the Introduction, I drew attention to an increasingly strident and often self-righteous moralism in public discourse; and the strident tone is often combined with a frustrating sense that compromise or rational resolution of disagreements is not possible. No doubt there are many reasons for this development. But strident self-righteousness seems like a natural outcome of the kind of frustration people feel when they find themselves unable to persuade by appeal to reason. I like to think that some of the ideas in this chapter and the one before may contribute to an understanding of why rational argument seems, at least in its first stages, ineffective.

One part of morality, certainly, has to do with what Hume calls "benevolence." When people argue for aid for the homeless, or for the victims of disease and natural disasters, they seek to engage our sympathy for someone suffering or in need. They appeal to our concern that others live well, or at least not in misery. And the arguments are often successful, at least in generating the sense that something ought to be done. But, when it comes to just how we ought to act, arguments of a very different kind are likely to appear. These arguments appeal to rights, rights of property, rights of privacy, rights arising out of contracts, or even just the vague idea that one has a right to be let alone and to make one's own decisions. One might say they are not so much about *what* to accomplish as about *how* to go about it. They may not tell us to abandon our projects or our attempts to do good, but they may tell us we cannot pursue our projects in certain ways. We may have to get someone's permission, to persuade someone else to cooperate, or to work within the democratic process.

When people wonder why they can't just go ahead on their own, doing what seems, after all, obviously to have good immediate consequences, the response may include--and not without reason--an appeal to some kind of universalization test: "What if everyone did that?" This is one of Kant's basic questions, of course, and it is also a natural move in arguments about the need to comply with the kinds of social rule that figure in Hume's account of the requirements of justice. Surely, there is *something* right about appealing to this question, yet as I have argued extensively, its results are often ambiguous. It can be used by people on both sides of numerous moral debates with apparently equal effectiveness. Obviously, something more needs to be said about when it is relevant and how it is to be used before we--*any* of us--can feel rationally justified in using it. But the inconclusiveness of tests like this is not the only source of unresolvable controversy. Another source is related to the distinction Hume suggests between the idea of morality as a form of benevolence and morality as respect for rights and rules.

I don't want to suggest that every difficult moral question involves a conflict between rights and human kindness (or, as Hume might put it, between justice and benevolence). Yet conflicts like this are all around. Certainly arguments about abortion sometimes pit a humanitarian concern for the plight of a woman in trouble against the abstract right of someone not yet born (and those opposed to abortion try to portray the concern for the fetus in humanitarian terms and the woman as callously standing on her rights). Arguments about the needs of the poor and ill for health care are met by arguments about the rights of hospitals and health care providers to determine how long they will work and for how much. Arguments that certain publications are cruel, unkind, or offensive to someone's sensibilities are met by arguments about rights to freedom of expression. And arguments for requiring motorcycle helmets to save lives are met by the claim that people have the right to choose their own risks.

Though he may have thought he could reconcile justice and benevolence, Hume was also aware that the two could come into conflict. To his credit, however, he never tried to argue that we ought to dispense with either one. Though he saw that respect for rights could conflict with our humanitarian impulses, he nevertheless maintained a healthy appreciation for the importance of rights and rules in the life of a society. For he saw, as Hobbes saw, that the very rules which seem, in individual cases, to conflict with the desire to do good must in general be followed if we are to avoid even greater costs. It is just a fact that we cannot recognize any rights without accepting the consequence that they will sometimes be exercised in ways that we don't like, and in ways that may even go contrary to the clear demands of compassion. This is true of property rights and rights to personal freedom just as much as it is true of rights like freedom of expression or the right to vote.

We can recognize this, and we can agree with Hume that respect for rights is an important part of morality, and we can still leave open the question of *which* rights people have or should have. If I am right in thinking that many modern ethical controversies involve clashes between rights and other moral concerns (or even between one putative right and another), then what rights people have becomes a crucial question. In discussing Aristotle, I noted that his approach to ethics, taking the perspective of a single individual, seems ill-suited to the task of showing which rights people have, since rights concern the distribution of freedom and authority among different people. Modern moral philosophy attempts to stand back from the perspective of a single person and assess actions and character from a more general point of view. But that idea, as it stands, is still too vague to resolve these issues. If we take it to mean just that we should be benevolent, seeking to advance the general welfare as much as possible, then we again encounter the problem that concern for rights and concern for welfare can actually conflict.   Kant's idea of the moral perspective seemed different, yet when applied to to the question of how one should act on specific occasions, it yielded no clear answer at all.   We are left, then, with two questions.   First, what rights do people have and how can they be justified?   Second, assuming that morality involves both a concern to promote well-being and a need for secure rights, how might these two parts of morality be related to one another?   In Chapter 6 I will explore an approach to answering both these questions.   First, though, in Chapter 5 I will discuss a theory that attempts to derive all of morality from the single concern of promoting welfare.   In both chapters I will emphasize the question of whether morality, as conceived in the theories discussed, can be justified *to* those who are asked to comply with it.

5

UTILITARIANISM

JEREMY BENTHAM, 1748-1832
JOHN STUART MILL, 1806-1873

For Jeremy Bentham and John Stuart Mill, much more than for Hume and Kant, the aim of moral philosophy is *practical.* They assume there is controversy about what morality requires, and they aim to instruct and persuade. In this respect, they differ from Hume. In Hume's view, there was no serious question about *what* morality required. He assumed there was general agreement, and he took the task of philosophy to be that of explaining why we hold these specific beliefs, why we agree to the extent we do, and how we come to care about morality and to do what it requires. He was not particularly concerned with persuading people to be moral, since he thought we care about it most of the time naturally. (Though when he says we behave morally because we are naturally benevolent, he also implies that we could justify its demands to people by appealing to their benevolent sentiments.)

Bentham and Mill, by contrast, are not nearly so optimistic about the natural tendency to behave morally, and neither do they think there is nearly so much agreement about what morality requires. So, it is not their aim to explain why we (supposedly) agree on certain moral requirements or how it is that we tend to comply with them. Their aim is to tell us what we really should be doing. They are not out to tell us what we do do, or why we do it, but to tell us what we would be morally *justified* in doing. Indeed, more generally, they want to tell us what, for anyone, would count as an adequate justification for doing one thing rather than another. This is the sense in which their work is practical. It is intended not to describe how we do choose but to guide us in our future choices. But unlike Kant, who was also concerned with how moral choices should be made and how they could be justified, Bentham and Mill do not assume they can find out how to do these things by uncovering a law or principle that is *already* implicit in our common moral understanding. In their view, we need to concentrate not on what we now believe or think to be right, but rather on what *is* right.

The idea they come up with, put briefly, is that we ought to act so as to promote as much happiness and as little unhappiness as possible. The best way to justify a course of action is to show that it produces more happiness than any alternative. To cause unhappiness for no purpose, or even to promote less happiness than we might, is to act in a way that cannot be justified.

On their face, these are attractive ideas. They tell us to pay attention to the actual good and bad consequences of what we propose to do and not be bound by rigid rules that serve no good human purpose. They have a natural appeal to anyone with a humane concern for human well-being. And Bentham and Mill meant to apply these ideas very broadly. The principle of utility, or, as they sometimes called it, the Greatest Happiness Principle, was meant to apply to personal decisions and also to social and political decisions. It was meant to tell us how to conduct our relations with family and friends, and also how to reform the tax code and the penal code, and even how to write a constitution. This latter point brings out an important fact about the utilitarians. Both Bentham and Mill wrote extensively about social and political issues. Bentham devised schemes for the reform of the penal code, which he regarded as harsh and inhumane; and Mill wrote famous works defending individual freedom and advocating the liberation of women. Both were social, political, and economic *reformers* who were moved by a humane concern to promote human well-being. They thought that society could be improved and so could our ideas about morality; and they thought the improvement of the latter would help improve the former. They thought much of traditional morality irrelevant, outmoded, and repressive.

Before exploring the utilitarian theory in more detail, it might be worthwhile to consider some parallels between utilitarianism and Kant's theory. Some writers emphasize the differences between the two. They say, in particular, that Bentham and Mill are concerned about promoting good consequences (happiness) and that Kant doesn't care at all about consequences. (Indeed, Mill himself suggests this contrast in the introduction to his *Utilitarianism.*) But I doubt that this is true. Granted, Kant says that a *desire* for good consequences is not the same as a morally good will. He also says that a person could be acting with a good will, and so be worthy of praise even if, due to bad luck, the act didn't have good consequences. But neither of these points implies that the consequences of an act have nothing to do with whether it is or would be the right thing to do. More important, focusing on this alleged disagreement about the relevance of consequences obscures some very important similarities between the two theories.

For Kant, the laws of morality are *categorical*. What that means is that they apply to us, regardless of our personal desires, plans, or projects. They aren't based on what we happen to want. They don't just tell us what we have to do to get what we want. They tell us what is *right*. There may well, if Kant is right, be a clash between what morality requires and what we want or even what is good for us. Morality is not likely to be comfortable or convenient. To the extent that we are not perfectly rational creatures, but are also people with desires and inclinations, morality does not come naturally to us.

Bentham and Mill would agree with this. They don't share Kant's idea that moral demands are, in some way, built-in requirements of reason that our own rational natures impose on us; but they do agree that there is a big difference between what we *ought* to do and what we want to do, what is convenient, what is customary, or even what is *thought* to be right. The business of moral philosophy is to tell us what *is* right and to show us why.

For Bentham and Mill, then, the aim of moral philosophy is to give us an account of how we ought to behave and to provide a rational justification for this account. But they do not think justifying a moral principle is a matter of showing that it accords with our preferences, promotes our aims, or is otherwise good for us. Instead, it requires showing that it is right from a moral point of view. They accept the modern idea, in common with other modern philosophers, that the moral point of view is different from an individual's point of view-- that it is, in some sense, impartial. But then, like all modern theories, theirs gives rise to the question of how the demands of morality can be justified *to* the particular individuals to whom they apply. How do these demands fit with our other interests, goals, and projects? What role or roles do they play in our lives? Are they entirely alien and even hostile to our interests?

WHAT THE PRINCIPLE OF UTILITY REQUIRES

Roughly speaking, utilitarianism requires that we bring about as much happiness as possible for as many people as possible. This much I have already said. As it stands, however, the principle is far from precise, and it is also not exactly what Bentham and Mill say. Indeed, they say a number of different things at different times. It is important that we be aware of the uncertainty about what the utilitarians intended, for reasons I will try to explain.

The idea that we should pay attention to the consequences of our actions and, in particular, that what we should do depends in some way on the happiness or unhappiness we might cause, is an immensely attractive idea. Much of the intuitive appeal of utilitarianism comes from its insistence on just this idea. But as it stands it is vague. In *what* way does happiness matter? *Whose* happiness? Is it more important to promote happiness or to prevent unhappiness? Is happiness the *only* thing that matters? Until we answer these questions, we have nothing more than an appealing, but vague, idea. The question is whether, when the idea is made more precise, it will still have its appeal. After all, a *specific* answer to these questions that seems right in some circumstances might seem terrible in other circumstances. Does Bentham or Mill ever offer a clear account of the principle of utility?

In the early pages of *The Principles of Morals and Legislation*,[1] Bentham says the principle of utility is "that principle which approves or disapproves of every action whatsoever, according to the tendency which it appears to have to augment or diminish the happiness of the party whose interest is in question." Sometimes, he indicates a little further down the same page, that party may be "the community in general," but sometimes "a particular individual" [2].

This principle is ambiguous in more than one way. Suppose we are faced with some decision, and neither of the possible actions is ideal: Each will cause some happiness for someone, and each will also cause some unhappiness. In that case, it appears, the principle of utility will both "approve" and "disapprove" of both actions. Each is right to some extent and wrong to some extent. What do we do? Perhaps someone will suggest that we should choose the action that is right to a greater extent, meaning the one that will cause the greater amount of happiness. But what if that act *also* produces greater unhappiness? (This could happen if there is more than one person involved, and if their desires are directly opposed. The more one is made happy, the more the other is made unhappy.) In that case, the act that is *better* also seems to be the act that is *worse*. The principle, as stated, does not give us a clear directive. Yet over eighty years later, John Stuart Mill, in *Utilitarianism*,[2] still sometimes characterizes the principle of utility in almost the same terms. "The Greatest Happiness Principle," he says, "holds that actions are right in proportion as they tend to promote happiness, wrong as they tend to produce the reverse of happiness" [7].

One problem, then, if we are to understand just what the principle of utility is supposed to require is to figure out how it can be formulated coherently, while still holding to the basic idea that the rightness or wrongness of acts is a function, respectively, of their tendency to promote happiness or unhappiness. But this is not the only problem with the passages from Bentham quoted above. Acts, he says, are right in proportion as they promote happiness, wrong in proportion as they promote the reverse for "the party whose interest is in question" or "the party whose interest is considered." How do we decide whose interest is in question? Could we legitimately decide, for example, to consider just our own?

On this issue, Mill is a good deal less ambiguous than Bentham. The standard of utility, Mill says, "is not the agent's own greatest happiness, but the greatest amount of happiness altogether" [11]. And he goes on to say, a little later, that "the happiness which forms the utilitarian standard of what is right . . . is not the agent's own happiness, but that of all concerned. As between his own happiness and that of others, utilitarianism requires him to be as strictly impartial as a disinterested and benevolent spectator." He even compares this ideal to the ideal of Jesus of Nazareth: "Love your neighbor as yourself" [17]. Though Mill speaks, like Bentham, of the happiness "of all concerned," he evidently means *anyone* who might be affected.

Perhaps this is also what Bentham means when he speaks of "the party whose interest is in question." As a matter of interpretation, I am not convinced one way or the other. At least when he is evaluating an action of a government (like passing a law), the standard Bentham means to apply is certainly "the interest of the *community*" [3, italics added]. And, if pressed, perhaps he would say, as Mill does, that what is always relevant is the interest of as wide a community as might be affected by any of the possible acts we face. Anyhow, in what follows I will adopt the modern interpretation of utilitarianism, according to which the rightness or wrongness of an act depends on its consequences for *everyone* affected. The relevant standard, on this view, is always the interest of the community of all those affected.

But what does it mean to speak of the interest of a community? This is just the kind of vague phrase that Bentham hated:

> The interest of the community is one of the most general expressions that can occur in the phraseology of morals: no wonder that the meaning of it is often lost. When it has a meaning, it is this. The community is a fictitious *body*, composed of the individual persons who are considered as constituting as it were its *members*. The interest of the community then is what?--the sum of the interests of the several members who compose it [3].

In Bentham's view, then, the interest of a group is just the sum of the interests of the individuals who compose it. And what is the interest of an individual? "A thing is said to promote the interest . . . of an individual when it tends to add to the sum total of his pleasures: or, what comes to the same thing, to diminish the sum total of his pains" [3]. An act accords with the principle of utility "when the tendency it has to augment the happiness of the community is greater than any it has to diminish it" [3].

Earlier, I complained that Bentham's principle was unclear because it seemed to have the consequence that some acts could be both right and wrong (given that an act might have both good and bad consequences). The passages just quoted clarify the principle, for now Bentham seems to say that an act is right if and only if it produces *more* happiness than unhappiness (taking into account the effects on everyone). However, this does not solve all problems. What i´ two alternative acts (e.g., two alternative bills in Congress) would ɔoth produce more happiness than unhappiness, but one would produce a greater *balance* of happiness over unhappiness? Or suppose we are in a bad situation, like a natural disaster, and no option will produce more happiness than unhappiness? All we can do is minimize losses. Shouldn't we do so? Is the principle of utility silent in this case?

Despite his dislike of vague and unclear ideas, Bentham is less than precise himself on these points. Yet his idea that the interest of the community is the sum of the interests of its members gives us a good clue as to how we might formulate a more precise interpretation of his principle: If the interest of the community is the sum of the interests of its members, then to act in the interest of the community is to act so as to *maximize* this sum. Since the interest of an individual is increased by pleasure or happiness and decreased by pain or unhappiness, we maximize the good of the community only when we maximize the sum of happiness minus unhappiness. In short, if we interpret unhappiness or pain as negative happiness, then what the principle of utility requires is that we maximize *net* happiness--happiness minus unhappiness.

This, then, is the way that I will interpret the principle of utility:

> An act is right if and only if it produces at least as much net happiness as any other alternative open to the agent at the time, where the happiness or unhappiness of everyone affected by any alternative is considered, and considered equally. (If, in some situation, all the alternatives yield negative net benefits, then the right one is the one that produces the least net harm.)

This formulation of the principle seems to capture the ideas, clearly present in both Bentham's and Mill's writings, that producing happiness counts in favor of an act, while producing unhappiness counts against it. It also picks up on the idea that the overall value of an act is to be determined by summing its consequences, both good and bad. Finally, the idea that the consequences for each should be weighed equally captures Mill's idea that utilitarianism requires an agent to be "as strictly impartial as a disinterested and benevolent spectator" [16]. Finally, though neither Bentham nor Mill actually formulates the principle in exactly this way, modern utilitarians do.

More than any other principle we have considered in this book, the principle of utility offers a precise account of how we ought to behave. True, it is hard to tell, most of the time, just how much happiness a given person will get from a given act. Indeed, there is a large technical literature on whether we can even make sense of this idea. But I am going to bypass this issue here. What I find significant is that we always know at least what would count for or against an act, according to utilitarianism. We know just where to look, and we know just what is relevant. And, sometimes, the consequences of the principle are obvious. For example, if there are two choices, and one is better for some people and no worse for any of the others, then it is definitely better from a utilitarian perspective.

The fact that the principle of utility sometimes offers clear and definite advice is surely one of the main reasons for its wide popularity today. The classical utilitarians, as I have already emphasized, were practical reformers who wanted to offer guidance to those in a position to make changes. Indeed, they worked closely with the economists of their day (Mill, the author of *Principles of Political Economy*, was an economist as well as a philosopher); and the general idea that economic institutions should be judged in terms of their overall contribution to individual well-being is still fundamental to most modern work in welfare economics.

Another reason for the popularity of utilitarianism is its basic humanism--its idea that what matters is preventing suffering and promoting well-being. What, after all, could be more important? Yet, as we shall see, there are powerful objections to utilitarianism even if there is also much to be said in its favor. Perhaps ironically, the very fact that the principle of utility is clear enough to yield some definite answers may help make it subject to effective criticism; it actually *says* something. Later on, I will have a lot to say about objections to the principle and about the arguments Bentham and Mill offer in its support. Before turning to this task, however, I want to say something about a point on which the two disagree.

MILL'S CRITIQUE OF BENTHAM

Born in 1748, Jeremy Bentham entered Oxford at the age of fifteen to study law. Rather than practicing law, however, he spent his life studying and advocating the reform of legal and political institutions according to the dictates of utility. In 1808, when John Stuart Mill was two years old, his father, James Mill, made the acquaintance of Bentham. Thereafter, Mill's family spent a great deal of time with Bentham and his other utilitarian followers. John Stuart Mill himself was raised and educated largely under the influence of Bentham. It is no accident that he became the next generation's chief spokesman for utilitarianism; and yet, on certain crucial points, he came to disagree with Bentham. Partly this was a matter of emphasis. While both philosophers were concerned to a considerable extent with issues of institutional reform--with law, politics, and economics--Mill was also preoccupied with questions of personal ethics and, in particular, with ideas about how one should conduct one's personal life. Indeed, even his work in political philosophy reflects this concern, for his book *On Liberty* consists largely of an argument that individuals need to be left free to decide what kind of life is best for them. And this idea, in turn, is rooted in Mill's ideas about what makes a life a good or happy life.

The utilitarian principle requires that we pursue happiness, both for people generally and for ourselves. But just how do we go about this? Bentham, when he talks about how, in detail, one should evaluate an act, offers a very specific account of just what elements make up pleasure (which he equates with happiness). In a section of *The Principles of Morals and Legislation* called "Value of a Lot of Pleasure of Pain, How to be Measured," Bentham offers a purely quantitative method for deciding what to do. One should ask whether the pleasures resulting from one's act are certain or uncertain, immediate or delayed, and then one should evaluate the pleasures themselves in terms of their intensity and their duration. The more intense or the longer, the better [29]. And that is it.

This is the doctrine which Mill found unsatisfactory. It seemed to him that there could be enjoyments that were intense and long lasting, but which were still not as good, for the person who experiences them, as other enjoyments. Mill did not think of this as a moral matter. He did not mean that there was something morally objectionable about intense pleasures. He just meant that they might not contribute as much to one's well-being as other pleasures. He tended to express this point in terms of the difference between *quality* of pleasure and *quantity*: "[S]ome *kinds* of pleasure are more desirable and more valuable than others. It would be absurd that while, in estimating all other things, quality is considered as well as quantity, the estimation of pleasures should be supposed to depend on quantity alone" [8]. What does Mill have in mind? Surprisingly, he does not give a lot of examples. Among higher-quality pleasures, he mentions intellectual pleasures (by which I suppose he means the pleasures of study and learning), music, and, somewhat quaintly, the exercise of moral virtues like kindness. About lower pleasures, he says even less. No doubt he thought of beer drinking in the pub, and no doubt also he would today include bowling, pool, sex, drugs, and rock music.

What makes the difference between pleasures of higher and lower quality? How can we tell which pleasures have higher quality? Mill's answer is that we need to ask someone who has experienced both:

> Of two pleasures, if there be one to which all or almost all who have experience of both give a decided preference, irrespective of any feeling of moral obligation to prefer it, that is the more desirable pleasure. If one of the two is, by those who are competently acquainted with both, placed so far above the other that they prefer it, even though knowing it to be attended with a greater amount of discontent, and would not resign it for any quantity of the other pleasure . . . we are justified in ascribing to the preferred enjoyment a superiority in quality [8-9].

Those who are acquainted with them, Mill goes on to say, always "give a most marked preference to the manner of existence which employs their higher faculties." "[N]o intelligent human being would consent to be a fool, no instructed person would be an ignoramus . . . even though . . . the fool . . . is better satisfied with his lot than they are with theirs" [9]. But this preference, Mill insists, is not a preference for less *happiness.* Anyone who thinks this "confounds the two very different ideas of happiness and content. . . . It is better to be a human being dissatisfied than a pig satisfied; better to be Socrates dissatisfied than a fool satisfied" [10].

These are big and controversial claims. They are interesting for more than one reason. In the context of this book, it is noteworthy that Mill, writing in the nineteenth century, is finally coming back to a question we have hardly mentioned since we left Aristotle. Kant, Hume, and Hobbes had very little to say about the nature of the good life, of human happiness or well-being. They thought it was important but, in their view, ethics had to do not with how to be happy or live well but mainly with how to behave toward others and how to achieve successful social cooperation. I suspect they thought it was obvious what individual happiness amounted to. But, for Mill, the question has become a real one again; and it is interesting that his answer actually sounds something like Aristotle's. Both believe that a happy life will involve the development and exercise of our "higher" faculties.

Still, Aristotle's discussion of this idea is much more sophisticated than Mill's. There are a number of points here. For one thing, while Aristotle thought a life was better if it included things like the exercise of intellectual abilities, he did not think of these as *replacing* other pleasures. In a way, he took more seriously than did Mill the idea that pleasures really differ in kind [Aristotle, 1175a, 22f]. While there is profound enjoyment in the "higher" pleasures, a complete life will include activities and pleasures of many different kinds. Indeed, there is a place for the most mundane amusements. They provide relaxation and restore us for our more intense pursuits [1176b, 9].

While Mill spoke of pleasures differing in kind, he also continued to speak of pleasure, or happiness (in the singular), as the good. Aristotle did not speak of pleasure as the good and, though he did call happiness the good, he also thought this was empty and uninformative. He thought the good life was pleasant, and he thought the pleasures of intellectual activity especially choiceworthy, but he thought it a mistake to say that pleasure is the good. One reason, already mentioned, was that he thought the pleasures of different activities to be different in kind. Another, and perhaps deeper reason, was that he thought of the good as what one should make one's aim. But, like Butler, he thought that if pleasure was one's only aim, one could not possibly achieve it. Pleasure is more like a by-product of other activities pursued for their own sake. In a good life, pleasure cannot be the only thing sought for its own sake. I think Mill was simply confused about this issue. In Chapter IV of *Utilitarianism* he claims that we seek, and should seek, many different things as ends in themselves, yet he also says that happiness is the sole thing desirable as an end and that the good is to be identified with what we seek as an end. His attempts to reconcile these claims are not convincing.

There is a further difference between Mill and Aristotle that needs to be mentioned. Aristotle, like the Greeks in general, takes it for granted that ethics is about the question of how one should live one's life, and he further assumes that this is the question of what one needs to do to live well or to be happy. He needs to investigate the nature of the good or happy life because he wants to tell people how they can achieve it in their own lives. But Mill, like other modern philosophers, sees moral philosophy as the study of how one should behave, not just in terms of one's own well-being, but from a viewpoint impartial among people in general. Following Bentham, he thinks this amounts to doing what maximizes net happiness overall. Thus, though the question "what is happiness?" plays a central role both in Aristotle's and in Mill's theories, each of them makes use of the answer in a very different way. As twentieth-century philosophers often put it, the two have similar conceptions of the good, but very different theories of what is *right*. For Mill, what is right is to promote maximum net happiness overall, not just one's own. Most modern discussions of utilitarianism focus on the theory of right action. Is this theory reasonable?

JUSTIFYING THE PRINCIPLE OF UTILITY

One strength of the principle of utility is that it seems to give clear and definite answers to a number of moral questions. Thus, for example, if there is a natural disaster, the principle quite clearly directs medical personnel to use scarce resources first on those who are most likely to benefit--to survive and live decent lives if treated. It says we should not waste resources on those who are beyond help or on those who will recover without immediate attention. Again, if we are devising a tax policy (like an income tax reform), we should adopt the policy that will produce the least possible unhappiness. Thus, if it is true that the wealthy gain less happiness from each additional dollar than the poor (each dollar means less to someone who already has a lot), then, other things being equal, taxes on the wealthy should be higher.

Obviously, there might be questions in a real case about just who will benefit most from treatment or about whether it is really true that the rich benefit less than the poor from a dollar at the margin of their income. The principle of utility, *all by itself*, never settles any question. What one should do always depends partly on nonmoral judgments about the actual effects of a policy and about the relative size of costs and benefits. (For example, in the case of tax policy, whether the wealthy should be taxed more than the poor depends partly on whether the poor will benefit more from the dollars, but also on whether high taxes for the wealthy will reduce economic incentives.) At least, though, the principle of utility tells us exactly what to focus on, what is relevant to making a decision. It does the same in a case in which we have to decide whether to continue life-prolonging treatment for a terminally ill patient. We should do so just as long as doing so produces greater net happiness for everyone affected than any alternative. Here again, of course, it may be hard to say just how much happiness or unhappiness is involved. "Quality of life" judgments will have to be made. But the principle does tell us what is relevant.

My question here, though, is whether the principle of utility itself is the right one. This question has been hotly debated for over a century and, for utilitarianism, it is *the* question. Why? Early in this chapter, I pointed out a similarity between the utilitarians and Kant. For each, the requirements of morality are categorical. They are thought of as requirements we have to follow; and we have to follow them just because they are right. Neither Kantians nor utilitarians make any effort to show that their principles are somehow natural for us in the sense that they grow out of our normal inclinations or motives. Neither tries to show that they serve our purposes as ordinary people who want to lead happy and satisfying lives. True, philosophers like Aristotle, and even Epictetus, would have admitted that the attitudes and character traits they recommended require some sacrifice on our part. But both were convinced that normally, overall, they were for our own good. Hobbes and Butler, though for very different reasons, thought the same. Hume thought morality couldn't be grounded in self-interest but, like Butler, he thought our capacities for sympathy and benevolence gave us a natural interest in morality.

Bentham and Mill, by contrast, do not try to show that following their principle is natural for us, or that it is good for us. Mill, indeed, sometimes seems to go out of his way to defend himself against the objection that utilitarianism is a selfish or egoistic doctrine: "I must again repeat, what the assailants of utilitarianism seldom have the justice to acknowledge, that the happiness which forms the utilitarian standard of what is right in conduct, is not the agent's own happiness, but that of all concerned" [Mill, 16]. So what they have to show is that their principle is the morally right principle--that its demands are demands we *ought* to follow, regardless of whether we want to or of whether they are good for us. But is this principle right?

I have mentioned, above, some of the things which it appears the principle of utility would require. For example, I said that in an emergency, when medical supplies are short, it would require us to use the supplies carefully, concentrating on those who can be significantly benefited and not on those who are beyond help. And, I must say, it seems hard to disagree. This means making some hard decisions, and it means some will have to suffer; but some will have to suffer regardless, and it seems best to help those who can benefit most from the help. I also said that in the case of someone who is terminally ill and who can no longer benefit from further life-prolonging treatment, utilitarianism would recommend stopping the treatment. Again, I suspect that this is a reasonable position, and I would not disagree.

There are other cases, however, in which the principle of utility would seem to require, or at least permit, things that some people would not accept. For example, nothing in the principle itself rules out using active means ("a lethal injection") to end the life of someone who is terminally ill and suffering pain or indignity. After all, the utilitarian might reason, death will be quicker and more painless this way, while merely discontinuing treatment might make for a slower and more painful process of death. Moreover, active euthanasia could save the family's resources, both financial and emotional. And, for a utilitarian, *all* these factors count. To take another example, utilitarians would approve of capital punishment--*if* it could be shown that its benefits, in terms of deterrence, outweighed its costs--and they would also approve not only of the right to have abortions but also of performing some abortions *if*, as must sometimes be true, the benefits to the pregnant woman and her family were greater than the potential happiness of the fetus.

Nobody needs to be told that these issues are controversial. I do not necessarily disagree with what the principle of utility says about them. But, obviously, some people would strongly disagree with any principle that permits capital punishment, under any circumstances; and, by the same token, some people would reject any principle that even considers abortion. Many people think that both of these things are just plain morally wrong. Of course, these people themselves might be wrong. Utilitarians think they are. Utilitarians do not reject morality. They just think they have found the *right* moral principle, and that the people who disagree are the ones who are wrong.

Who is correct? This is the issue for utilitarians since, as I have claimed, they do not try to show that their principle has anything else going for it other than that it is right. It is not meant to be good advice for someone who wants to be happy, for example. It is meant to be a categorical demand. So how did Mill and Bentham try to show that their principle is the right one?

Mill gives an argument for the principle in Chapter IV of *Utilitarianism*. It is remarkable for how little it actually proves. What Mill actually argues is that people desire happiness, and that happiness is all that they desire, at least as an end. He admits that there are many other things that we want, but he claims that we want them as means to happiness or, when we like them for themselves, we desire them "as *part* of happiness" [36]. He then concludes that since we seek happiness and only happiness for its own sake, happiness and only happiness must be the good. Since we desire happiness, "happiness is a good . . . each person's happiness is a good to that person, and the general happiness, therefore, a good to the aggregate of all persons" [34].

There are a number of things that might be said about this argument. For one thing, as I have already noted, there is a problem about whether Mill's various claims here are even consistent: He wants to say both that happiness is all we desire as an end *and* that we desire many different things for their own sake. Indeed, Butler would object strenuously to the very idea that happiness or pleasure could be the sole thing we desire as an end. (If it were, what would we then do?) But that is not the issue I find most troubling in the present context. Mill indicates, in the title of Chapter IV, that he is concerned with finding a proof of the "principle of utility." But, what he actually discusses is not what we have called "the principle of utility"--the principle that one ought to act so as to maximize overall happiness-- but rather the idea that happiness is what is good for people. Yet these are separable ideas. Let me explain.

We can think of utilitarianism as being composed of two ideas. The first is the idea that what is good for people is their own happiness. (This is sometimes called the utilitarian "theory of the good," and it is an idea common to many theories, including Aristotle's.) The second is the idea, which I have called the principle of utility, that tells us that what we *ought* to do is to try to maximize total, net happiness overall. (This is the utilitarian "theory of the right.") It is certainly possible to believe the first of these ideas but not the second. Aristotle did. (He sometimes suggests, in his *Politics*, that government should be arranged to make possible good lives for everyone capable of leading them; but there is no idea here of *maximizing* the good, no suggestion that we act wrongly if we fail to produce the most possible happiness.) It is even possible to believe, as Mill asserts, that the general happiness is good for the aggregate of persons, without believing that what any one of us must (or even may) do is to promote the good of the aggregate. Why doesn't Mill ever attempt to justify the utilitarian theory of the right?

I can only speculate, but perhaps, as he and Bentham saw it, the idea that happiness is good seemed so radical all by itself that the question of the correctness of the maximizing principle seemed, by comparison, a trivial detail. There is some evidence for this interpretation in Mill's text. According to Mill, the "theory of life" on which utilitarianism is grounded is the theory "that pleasure and freedom from pain are the only things desirable as ends" [7]. When Mill considers objections to utilitarianism, most of the objections he mentions are all directed at this "theory of life." The idea that pleasure is the good, Mill has his critics say, is "a doctrine worthy only of swine" [7]. Mill's reply, quite in keeping with his critique of Bentham, is to insist that the idea that pleasure is the good does not mean that only the "lower" pleasures are good.

A few pages later, Mill characterizes the Greatest Happiness Principle as the principle that "the ultimate end . . . for the sake of which all other things are desirable . . . is an existence exempt as far as possible from pain, and as rich as possible in enjoyments . . ." [11]. Again, he considers objections, but the objections have to do with whether happiness is even possible, and whether it would be good even if we had it, and he replies by explaining further how he conceives of happiness [12f]. He then goes on to consider what he sees as Stoic ideas to the effect that one sometimes needs to rise above one's desires for happiness, cultivate attitudes that lead to tranquility, or even sacrifice one's own happiness. He does not deny that such ideas are sometimes correct, but he insists that when they are, it is only because self-renunciation is sometimes a good means to securing one's own long-term happiness or the greater happiness of another. What he sees as the doctrine to be denied is the doctrine that self-renunciation might in some way be good *in itself*, even when it makes no contribution to happiness [16].

These passages are revealing. They indicate something about what Bentham and Mill thought themselves to be doing and how they saw their adversaries. In their minds, what was revolutionary about utilitarianism was the idea that individual happiness is good and that pointless self-sacrifice was just that--pointless. This idea comes out clearly again if we look back at Chapter II of Bentham's *Principles of Morals and Legislation*. That chapter is evidently meant to be Bentham's main argument in favor of the principle of utility. The Chapter is titled "Of Principles adverse to that of Utility," and the idea seems to be that if these are wrong, then the principle of utility is the only reasonable alternative. But Bentham considers only two alternatives. One he calls the "principle of asceticism" [8f], and the other he calls the "principle of sympathy and antipathy" [13f]. The latter, he goes on to say, is really no principle at all. It just amounts to deciding what to do by "intuition," or "gut reaction"; and that amounts, I suspect Bentham thought, to being ruled, thoughtlessly, by the haphazard accidents of cultural influence, religious training, or upbringing.

The principle of asceticism, on the other hand, is a definite principle. It amounts to the principle of utility turned on its head. Like the principle of utility, it has to do with happiness and unhappiness, "but in an inverse manner: approving of actions in as far as they tend to diminish . . . happiness; disapproving of them in as far as they tend to augment it" [9].

Needless to say, Bentham finds this principle utterly absurd, but what is significant is that he mentions it at all. Like Mill after him, he evidently thought his opponents regarded self-sacrifice, self-denial, and even suffering as good in themselves. Against the background of an assumption like this, it will seem revolutionary indeed just to assert that individual happiness is a good and desirable thing.

Two points need to be made here. First, even if we agree that individual happiness is good--indeed, even if we agree that it is the only intrinsically good thing--it does not follow at all that we ought to make all our decisions by asking what would maximize total happiness for people in general. Second, even if Bentham is right that the two alternatives he considers, the principle of asceticism and the principle of sympathy and antipathy, are wrong, we are not left with the utilitarian maximizing principle as the only alternative. Others, quite compatible with the idea that happiness is the good, are possible.

Bentham and Mill, then, offer arguments in support of the idea that happiness or pleasure are good; but they offer almost no support for the principle that we ought to try to maximize total happiness. Yet this idea is a *radical* idea. Looked at one way, it seems to demand a tremendous amount. In deciding what to do, according to this principle, we need to consider not just our own well-being, or the well-being of family and friends, but the well-being of everyone who might be affected by our choices. Moreover, we need not only avoid things that could cause harm or injury, but we need also to consider how we might be able to benefit people positively--*all* people. The principle says, after all, that we ought to *maximize total* happiness. A well-known article by Peter Singer, a modern utilitarian philosopher, makes it clear just what this commitment involves. His article is called "Famine and Affluence,"[3] and it makes the case not just that wealthy members of society ought to share with their less wealthy neighbors, but further that affluent societies ought to reduce their standard of living significantly in order to help those in impoverished countries in the third world. Singer makes the standard utilitarian argument that, at our level of affluence, additional dollars simply buy far less happiness than the same dollars would buy for people in abject poverty.

Again, I do not necessarily disagree with Singer's conclusion. I too believe wealthy nations consume more than their share and ought to give more aid to poorer nations. I merely wish to stress that the principle of utility really can demand substantial sacrifice. Yet, paradoxically, the principle of utility sometimes seems to demand of people far less than "traditional" morality demands. We have already seen, for example, that the principle would probably approve of rights to abortion and, at least in some cases, of euthanasia. The reason it might approve of these things is the *same* as the reason that it sometimes seems to make excessive demands. The principle of utility tells us to consider the effects of our actions on everyone, and it says that *every* benefit counts in favor of an act, and *every* cost against it. Just as the interests of people in distant countries can tip the scales in favor of some policy, so also, in a decision concerning the termination of a pregnancy or of life support, the interests of family and friends can tip the scales in favor of abortion or euthanasia. Since my own interests count, when these outweigh the interests of others, I can indulge myself. Since the interests of everyone else count, too, when theirs outweigh mine, I must sacrifice everything for them.

Utilitarian morality differs, then, from the ideas many people have about what morality requires. In some cases, it seems to demand a great deal; in other cases, it seems quite permissive. But none of this shows that it is wrong. Bentham and Mill were well aware that their theory might have radical implications. They thought of themselves as moral reformers. Yet, as I have argued, their attempts to show that their principle is actually right are inadequate. Modern utilitarians can offer further arguments in support of their principle. They can stress, as I already have, that it is clear and theoretically simple: It consists of a single rule that, in principle, can settle any controversy. They can also stress its flexibility: It recognizes that the circumstances in which we live and make our choices vary constantly, and the principle of utility requires us to take into account the circumstances that might affect the consequences of our acts. It never says that we *must* or *can't* do certain things regardless of the consequences. Finally, the principle of utility is humane. It is concerned with promoting human well-being, and with avoiding pain and suffering.

Surely, it is a good thing in a moral theory to be flexible and humane. But utilitarianism is by no means the only theory that has these properties. It is, remember, a very specific theory. It says that one ought always to do what will *maximize total* net happiness, considering the happiness or unhappiness of *everyone* who might be affected by what one does. It implies that one may, and even should, harm some people if that is necessary to produce a greater sum of happiness. (As noted above, there are utilitarian arguments for capital punishment, and there could well also be utilitarian arguments for, say, conducting risky medical experiments that would benefit the many at the expense of the few.) Utilitarianism cares only about the total quantity of happiness, not about how it is distributed. If the total will be greater in a world in which some suffer, that is still better, according to utilitarians, than a world with a smaller total in which no one suffers. Utilitarianism requires that we maximize total happiness, taking everyone into account. That is very different from making everyone happy.

Once we see this point, it is not hard to imagine possible alternatives to this theory that can still claim to be flexible and humane. For example, we might imagine a two-part theory that says something like this: First, see to it that people suffer as little harm as possible; and second, subject to that constraint, maximize happiness. Or, to take another example, instead of doing whatever would maximize total well-being, we might try to ensure that as many people as possible are happy to some reasonable degree.

I do not mean to claim that either of these principles is without its problems. In very unfortunate circumstances, for example, the decision absolutely to minimize harm might leave us with no attractive alternatives. And, of course, if we seek simply to see that as many people as possible achieve some level of happiness, we face the difficult problem of deciding just what this level should be. But my aim is not to defend these principles. It is simply to point out that, for someone who agrees with the basic utilitarian idea that human happiness is important, and pain and suffering bad, there are possible moral principles other than the simple one that requires us to maximize the total quantity of happiness no matter what. We can agree with utilitarian judgments about what is good, and still consistently adopt a different idea of what is morally right. Thus, even if we accept the utilitarian arguments to the effect that happiness is the good, that does not show that the principle of utility is the correct principle of morality. Yet, if I have been right, that is what utilitarians must show. What they claim for their principle is not that it is good for us, not that it is natural for us, but just that it is correct.

In the next chapter, I will devote more time to describing and defending an alternative to utilitarianism. Before doing so, however, I wish to return again to the theme I have pursued throughout the preceding chapters, namely, if we were to assume that utilitarianism is correct about what morality requires, then what possible reasons or motives would people have to be moral?

WHY DO WHAT UTILITARIANISM REQUIRES?

For people who are already committed to doing whatever is morally right, and who are also convinced that the utilitarian principle is the correct principle of morality, this question does not need any further discussion. The arguments we have considered, however, certainly do not show that utilitarianism is correct. Moreover, even if it is in some sense a true moral principle, not everyone is committed to doing whatever morality requires. What independent reason might people have for doing what utilitarianism requires? How do the requirements of a moral view like utilitarianism fit into interests, plans, and projects people normally have? Mill addresses this question directly, and Bentham addresses it indirectly. Their answers are very different. Indeed, they are close to contradictory. I will begin with Mill.

Chapter III of Mill's *Utilitarianism* is called "Of the Ultimate Sanction of the Principle of Utility." Any moral theory, Mill begins by saying, owes us an answer to the question "what is its sanction?"; and he means by this question "what are the motives to obey it?" [26]. Mill readily admits that people are not likely to feel a direct, natural motive to do what utilitarianism demands. "[C]ustom and education," he says, make most of us feel "bound not to rob, murder, deceive or betray"; but we do not similarly feel bound to promote the general happiness [26]. Still, he thinks, utilitarianism is no worse off, in this regard, than any other theory. "The principle of utility either has, or there is no reason why it might not have, all the sanctions which belong to any other system of morals" [27]. Why does he think this?

In general, Mill says, there are two possible kinds of sanction, or motive, for obeying any moral principle. He calls them "internal" sanctions and "external" sanctions. External sanctions consist mainly of social pressure from others, anything from fear of legal punishment to subtle expressions of pleasure or displeasure from friends and neighbors. If the members of our community believe in a moral principle, they will pressure us to follow it.

The second kind of motive, the internal sanctions, come from our own conscience, our own feeling of horror at doing what we take to be wrong. The force of conscience amounts to "a mass of feeling which must be broken through in order to do what violates our standard of right" [28]. It is this mass of feeling, conscience, which Mill calls the "ultimate sanction" [28] of any morality. But why should we believe that our "consciences" will make us want to be utilitarians--to strive to maximize the general happiness no matter what? Mill's basic answer is that conscience depends on education, on how we are brought up. The moral training people have received in the past has not left them with utilitarian consciences. Still, he says, "No reason has ever been shown why [feelings of obligation] may not be cultivated to as great intensity in connection with the utilitarian, as with any other rule of morals" [28].

So, Mill's general idea seems to be that whether people will actually be moral, or feel that they have a reason to do so, always depends on how they are brought up (as well as on "external sanctions," like pressure from others). People will be motivated to follow the principle of utility if they are brought up to do so, just as they will follow other principles if they are taught those instead.

In some ways, this idea may remind us of Aristotle's ideas about morality. Aristotle never claims that the moral virtues are something people will develop naturally. He explicitly denies this. Whether we are virtuous depends on how we are raised. However, there is this difference. Aristotle at least claims that we, or those who care about us, also have an independent reason to see to it that we develop the virtues. He claims that we benefit from having the virtues in the sense that people who have them live happier lives as a result. And I gave arguments to try to show that Aristotle is right about this. But Aristotle's virtues, traits like courage, temperance, and justice, do not seem to be the same as the requirement that one seek to maximize general happiness. Does Mill give us any reason to think that "utilitarian virtue" contributes to our own well-being in the same way? Does he give us any reason to think utilitarian attitudes fit naturally with any of our other, ordinary motives?

If anything, it appears that the requirements of utility conflict quite drastically with our ordinary motives. Indeed, Mill seems to admit this. We will not feel bound by the demands of utilitarianism, he says, "until, by the improvement of education, the feeling of unity with our fellow creatures shall be (what it cannot be denied that Christ intended it to be) as deeply rooted in our character, and to our own consciousness as completely a part of our nature, as the horror of crime is in an ordinary well brought up young person" [26]. To have the kind of attitude that would naturally lead us to act on the principle of utility, Mill says here, we would have to feel totally at one with all our "fellow creatures." And this is an idea he repeats more than once. In a passage already quoted, describing what utilitarianism requires of a person, Mill said, "[a]s between his own happiness and that of others, utilitarianism requires him to be as strictly impartial as a disinterested and benevolent spectator" [16]. And finally, at the end of the chapter on sanctions, Mill speaks again of the idea that we "generate in each individual a feeling of unity with all the rest; which, if perfect, would make him never think of, or desire, any beneficial condition for himself, in the benefits of which they are not included" [32].

What Mill acknowledges in these passages is that the principle of utility sets a very high standard indeed. It tells us, after all, to be prepared to sacrifice our own well-being, or that of others we care for, whenever doing so will produce some increase in total happiness. And it seems to me right, as Mill suggests, that we will not be naturally motivated to do this unless we have come to feel a complete unity with everyone, so that we care only about total happiness and are indifferent as to who, in particular, has it. If it is true that most ordinary people, even people we think quite moral, feel a primary concern for their own happiness or that of their friends and loved ones, then most people are a long way from the utilitarian ideal. It seems unlikely that developing utilitarian attitudes could be recommended to them as Aristotelian virtues--traits that would contribute to their own good.

I don't mean to suggest by this last remark that Mill thinks utilitarian attitudes particularly conducive to our own good. Indeed, he thinks they have a chance of taking hold mainly because there is "a natural basis of sentiment for utilitarian morality" in the form of "the social feelings of mankind" [30]. Like Hume and Butler, Mill thinks that people are not, by nature, purely selfish. They are naturally social; they sometimes voluntarily cooperate with others and take an interest in the interests of others. And I think Mill, like Hume and Butler, is entirely right about this. Neither Hume nor Butler, though, comes anywhere close to suggesting that our natural benevolence amounts to a total identification of our own interests with those of others. Indeed, ordinary benevolent motives are quite specific. We feel compassion, for example, for particular persons when we become aware of their suffering. Yet that kind of particular concern for a particular person's plight is just the sort of thing that could *prevent* us from doing what utilitarianism demands. For utilitarianism demands that we promote total happiness, even when this requires that we sacrifice the happiness of some particular person. It requires that we be *rational* in the promotion of aggregate happiness. Thus, for example, in caring for the injured after a natural disaster, it tells us to treat not those who may most engage our sympathy, but those who have the best objective chance of benefiting from the care we can give.

With the possible exception of Kant's theory, most of the others we have considered seem to begin with a picture of our normal concerns and attitudes, and then they proceed to show how moral or ethical requirements might promote these, or grow out of them. Utilitarianism, by contrast, begins with an abstract ideal, a demand that we maximize total well-being, and then casts about for possible motives to comply with it. As even Mill concedes, though, this ideal represents a demanding standard. He thinks it attainable, but I am not convinced. If I am right, we commit ourselves to a standard like this only at the cost of alienating ourselves from many of our ordinary concerns, including some of the concerns that people normally consider morally good.

Before concluding this section, however, I should say something about Bentham's views on the motives for following the principle of utility. Does he give us any more reason than Mill does to think that normal people have a reason for acting as the principle of utility requires? The short answer is "no." Still, what he does say contributes to an understanding of utilitarianism.

He begins *The Principles of Morals and Legislation* as follows: "Nature has placed mankind under the governance of two sovereign masters, *pain* and *pleasure*. It is for them alone to point out what we ought to do, as well as to determine what we shall do" [1]. How should we understand this passage? Certainly, at the beginning, it seems to be a remark about what motivates people. What leads us to act, Bentham says, is either the desire for pleasure or the desire to avoid pain; and these are *sovereign* masters. They are the only motives we have. Unlike Hume and Butler, but like Kant (at least when he is talking about our ordinary, affective nature), Bentham thinks we are self-interested pleasure seekers.

Suppose Bentham is right. What does that say about utilitarianism? Perhaps the idea that people strive for pleasure helps to support the claim that pleasure is (at least part of) the good for people; and this is certainly one of the things utilitarians are anxious to assert. (It is what Mill thinks he needs to show in his attempt to establish the principle of utility in Chapter IV.) But the utilitarian theory of right action says not that we ought to seek our own pleasure or happiness but that we ought to maximize the general happiness. Since it is perfectly possible that maximizing total happiness can conflict with promoting our own, Bentham's theory suggests that our natural motives are in serious conflict with the demands of morality. Our natural desires lead us to seek our own pleasure, but morality requires that we promote the pleasure of people in general. Hence, on Bentham's theory, our natural motives give us very little reason to be moral. That does not mean Bentham is wrong about what morality requires, but it emphasizes one of the similarities between his theory and Kant's. For Kant also saw a deep conflict between our natural motives, as affective creatures, and the categorical demands of morality.

Bentham and Mill did not set out to tell us what we naturally want to do, but what we morally ought to do. If Bentham is right about our natural motives, then it is likely that we have little natural motivation to do what he thinks we ought to do. Had he appreciated the arguments of Butler and Hume, he might have adopted a theory of motivation that would make for less potential conflict between natural motives and the demands of utilitarianism. But Bentham takes a different approach. He grants that we have little natural reason to act as utilitarianism requires. He then concludes that the task of government is to establish institutional arrangements that artificially lead people to act so as to maximize utility. (Bentham's book, remember, is called *The Principles of Morals and Legislation*.) He views the criminal law, the tax code, and the market economy as systems of incentives and disincentives that lead us to act in ways that will promote the general utility. These institutions can make my own self-interest coincide with the *general* interest.

CONCLUSION: SHOULD WE BE UTILITARIANS?

While Bentham emphasizes the power of institutional arrangements to motivate behavior, and Mill emphasizes the power of education, both believe that the requirements of morality, as *they* see them, are likely to be in conflict with our normal motives and interests. This conflict is a consequence partly of the nature of the principle of utility, and partly, especially in the case of Bentham, of specific assumptions about our normal motives. To begin with, the principle of utility sets a very high standard of conduct. In demanding that we act, always, in a way that will produce as much total well-being as possible, it may well require us to sacrifice our own interests or those of our friends and loved ones. And it may even require that we act against ordinary motives of sympathy and compassion. The demands of utility can conflict with our ordinary motives, then, whether or not we are purely self-interested. But if, as Bentham claims, we are motivated solely by desires for pleasure and the avoidance of pain, conflicts are even more likely.

I have mentioned analogies between the utilitarian conception of morality and Kant's. Both share the idea that the demands of morality are categorical, in the sense that they apply to people whether or not they have any natural interest in complying. A second analogy, at least between Kant and Bentham, is that both think people are basically self-interested hedonists, seeking only to promote their own pleasure and to avoid pain or discomfort. It is almost as if, just because both have a low estimate of our natural motives, both are led to invest the demands of morality with great importance. However, just because both think we are (largely) selfish, each has a difficult problem seeing how we could ever be motivated to act as morality requires. But here their theories diverge. Bentham focuses on the power of society and government to provide external incentives for moral behavior, while Kant postulates (without adequate evidence) the idea of our own reason as a kind of internal government imposing internal sanctions on immoral behavior.

Most of us, of course, are accustomed to the idea that moral requirements sometimes conflict with what we would otherwise want to do. The fact that utilitarianism makes categorical demands, then, certainly does not show that it is wrong, that it does not give a correct picture of what morality requires. On the other hand, neither do the arguments of Bentham and Mill show that utilitarianism is correct. From the beginning of this book, I have focused on the way morality sometimes appears to people as an alien burden, and I have taken the attitude that burdens like this need not be heeded unless they can be justified, and justified in ways that make sense to the people they apply to. The mere *assertion* that something is required by morality is never enough.

The utilitarians would have agreed. They saw themselves as offering an alternative to the dogmatic moralists of their own time, an alternative that was humane and reasonable--an alternative that could be justified to the people who are asked to obey it. In a long footnote to Chapter II of *The Principles of Morals and Legislation*, Bentham acknowledges that people have different ideas about morality, and that these may derive from sources other than the principle of utility. He does not pretend that utilitarianism is the only conception of morality we can imagine. He does insist, though, that only utilitarianism "can properly be justified . . . by a person addressing himself to the community" [19, fn. 9]. In my view, this is the right test for a moral view--whether it can be defended to the community that is expected to live under it. What has not been shown, however, is that utilitarianism passes the test.

It is true that utilitarianism *aims* at promoting human happiness and, in that sense, it has a natural appeal. But, as I have argued above, promoting maximum total happiness is not the same as promoting the happiness of everyone. The share of some, indeed, may be very low. That is why I doubt that utilitarianism can, in fact, be adequately justified by "a person addressing himself to the community." At least, it cannot be justified adequately "to the community" if this means "to every member of the community, in terms that each can be expected to find acceptable."

PART THREE

Contemporary Reflections

6

A CONTRACTUALIST FRAMEWORK FOR MORALITY

I began this book by commenting on the moralistic tone of contemporary public discourse. When we aren't busy claiming moral rights for ourselves, we are busy insisting on higher standards of conduct for others. There is no shortage of people who think they know what is right and who are anxious to impose their standards on others. And most of us buy into this. If we are not active participants in the moral debates, we at least aren't indifferent to whether we manage to live morally decent lives ourselves.

The question I have stressed is whether people really have good reason to take the demands of morality seriously. Does morality serve an important function in our lives as individuals, or in the life of our community? If so, what is this function, and is it something that normal men and women, with normal interests and aims, have a reason to care about?

Sophisticated people, after all, sometimes take a cynical attitude toward morality. They say it is arbitrary, oppressive, and sometimes emotionally disastrous for anyone who takes it seriously. True, people who talk this way usually do think there are some important rules, like rules against violence and assault. And, it may also be true that, today, the trend is in the other direction, with most people decrying what they call "permissiveness" and calling for "higher moral standards." I am convinced, though, that some people do suffer because their lives are too dominated by judgments and evaluations, by "shoulds" and "oughts," and by high expectations for themselves. But this is not enough to convince me that there aren't important moral or ethical standards, that they don't play a beneficial role in our own lives and our communities. The question is *which* standards are important and reasonable, and how we can best come to appreciate the good they do for us. For standards that don't serve a good purpose do not deserve our attention.

In the preceding chapters, we have discussed a number of different philosophers. We have looked at their ideas both about what morality is and about what it requires. We have also looked at their ideas about what people are like, what their normal aims, purposes, and motives are. All believe that there is such a thing as morality or ethics, and all believe that it can require us to alter our attitudes or motives, to behave differently from the way we are sometimes motivated to behave. All think there are good reasons why we should limit our pursuit of what we take to be our immediate self-interest. Beyond that there are many differences. Conceptions of morality range from Epictetus's idea that people need to limit desires and lower expectations in the interest of their own happiness to Mill's and Bentham's idea that people should seek to maximize total happiness overall or Kant's idea that people should do only what could be willed as a universal law.

Accounts of human motivation range from Hume's and Butler's idea that people have a great variety of natural desires, including a natural concern for the interests and well-being of others, to Bentham's idea that "[n]ature has placed mankind under the governance of two sovereign masters, *pain* and *pleasure*." Then there is the idea, in Epictetus and Aristotle, and also in Mill, that people are capable of developing very different kinds of character and interests, depending on their upbringing. Finally, there is Kant's idea that our affective motives--our desires, inclinations, and emotions--are all self-interested, but that we have a separate source of motivation, in the form of laws of reason, that motivates us to do what reason and morality require.

The philosophers we have discussed disagree about whether there *should* be a close connection between the requirements of morality and what we are normally motivated to do. Some, like Hume, believe there must be, for otherwise we could not explain the fact that people do, in fact, try to act morally and to get others to do the same. Others, like Kant and the utilitarians, are struck by the fact that there is bound to be some difference between what people *do* and what they *ought* to do. Morality is, after all, something like a code of *ideal* behavior, and so we should expect to find a conflict between what morality requires and what we ordinarily want to do. Morality doesn't tell us what we want to do, or what is convenient; it tells us what is *right*. If something is right, that is all we need to know. We know we must do it, whether or not it is consistent with our other aims. Period.

This is not the position I take. In my view, nothing is *just* right. What is right or good, in my view, is right or good relative to some standard or purpose. The right solution to a math problem, the right wine for a meal, or the right way to dress for a formal occasion are all right because they meet standards or requirements of some particular kind. When something is *morally* right, it satisfies a *moral* standard. But given that something is right--that it satisfies a certain requirement, passes a certain test, or whatever--it can still be appropriate to ask whether there is any reason to care about the fact that it is right. I am sure that a Phillips screwdriver is the *right* tool for turning a Phillips head screw. But this is of little interest to me if I am confronted with an ordinary, slotted screw. It may be that giving a student a second chance on an exam would be the *best* thing for that student; but that does not settle the question of what I should do if I also want to be fair to the other students.

If I know that something is right, I know there is some standard relative to which it is the thing to do or to choose. Knowing that it is right helps me decide what to do, *if* that standard is the right standard. Whether it is or is not right depends on needs and purposes and other factors that can vary with the circumstances.

Why should we think it is any different for the standards of morality? Someone will say, no doubt, that the standards of morality are important, and are *always* important, whereas what is best for a Phillips screw, or for a particular person, is not always so important. And perhaps this is true. But if morality is always important in this way, then it should be possible to show this, and what I am asking is how it can be shown. This attitude toward morality is akin to the attitude of seventeenth- and eighteenth-century liberals toward the state: Just as the demands of the state need to be justified *to* those who are subject to its authority, so also the demands of morality need to be justified to those *to* whom they apply.

When Kant claims that the demands of morality are the same as the demands of reason and that we are truly free only when we act out of respect for those demands, he means to portray morality's demands as attractive and compelling. He is trying to answer the question "why be moral?" The same is true when Butler or Hume, in a very different way, try to show that we all have benevolent motives, that morality tells us to act on these motives, and that acting on these motives may well promote our own self-interest. But I have expressed doubts about all these claims. I don't think Kant succeeds in showing that the demands of morality are the demands of freedom, and I also don't think he even succeeds in explaining clearly just what the demands of morality are. Again, though I agree with Butler and Hume that people have numerous natural motives other than simple self-interest, and that these include benevolence, I believe they fail to show that what is morally required is the same as what is benevolent. As Hume himself notes, morality includes justice, and justice sometimes conflicts with benevolence.

Bentham and Mill, though they think the demands of morality conflict both with self-interest and with customary ideas of what is moral, oddly enough devote little effort to showing why we should care about these demands. They think we can be educated to care about them, and that the law can provide us with artificial incentives to comply with them. But this just pushes the question of justification one step back. If acting like a utilitarian has no natural appeal to me, why would I want to be pushed or prodded or indoctrinated into caring about it? If I do not think it does my children any good to be utilitarians, why should I want to raise them to have utilitarian motives?

For those who are concerned with the question "why be moral?" it is necessary to think not only about what morality might be thought to require but also about what kinds of interests and motives people normally have. More important, we should not look at one of these questions in isolation from the other. Rather, as we look at one, we need to have an eye on the other. Our question needs to be something like this:

> Is there some conception of morality, *together with* a plausible conception of normal human interests and motives, such that the demands of morality, on this conception, can be justified to people who have those interests?

This question sets the agenda for the rest of this chapter. Before proceeding, however, we need to consider a few assumptions and qualifications.

First, though the issue is how moral requirements can be justified to people, I do not assume it will be possible to justify all requirements to everyone. What particular people are interested in, or moved by, I believe, depends partly on upbringing and personal experience. While it is true that some moral traits, like courage and self-control, are useful in virtually any way of life; and while it is also true that attitudes of concern and respect for others foster many kinds of happy life, the fact remains that some people have interests and attitudes that conflict with reasonable moral demands and lack concerns that would make those requirements reasonable *for them*. Children raised in deprived circumstances may never dare to hope for some of the things that, in turn, would make an investment in Aristotelian virtues worthwhile.

For them, stealth and cunning may be more valuable than prudence and a sense of fair play. And people in the professional classes, isolated in homogeneous subdivisions and having no contact with the poor, may lose their capacity to sympathize with anyone unlike themselves. Kant seemed to assume that morality, if there is such a thing at all, is something that everyone, necessarily, has a reason to follow. Either everyone was rationally committed to the categorical imperative or there was no morality at all. But I see no reason to make that assumption.

Second, we needn't assume that morality, to be worth caring about, needs to be justified to people in terms of interests that are somehow natural. Most of the interests we have, from our taste in food to our hobbies or our love for our families, are interests we acquire. They develop over a period of time. (When I was a child, for example, pizza was not widely available. I was in my early teens before I ever tried it, and it took me a while to get used to it. Now, it would be hard to live without it.) The point is that what is good for us, even what seems essential, is by no means to be identified with what is natural, innate, or basic. Certainly Aristotle would agree; and so, for different reasons, would Epictetus. Neither thinks living well is just a matter of doing one's best to satisfy whatever desires one happens to have at the time. Each thinks it is partly a matter of having the right desires, and both think that that may mean changing or developing new desires. For Aristotle, whether we live well depends on how we are raised. A person who lives well is a person who has acquired the right desires and interests and who lives accordingly. We shouldn't be surprised if some of our interest in morality stems from interests we acquire through our upbringing. Indeed, these acquired interests may also be the source of our most profound satisfactions.

Finally, as I approach the question "why be moral?" I do not assume that "morality" (or "ethics") refers to any *one* thing. One reason for reading the history of moral philosophy is to remind ourselves of the different ways in which ethics might be conceived. We have encountered perhaps three different conceptions in this book. First, there is the Greek idea that ethics is concerned with the attitudes and character traits we need to develop if we are to live good and happy lives. Second, there is the idea, most prominent in people like Hume and Butler, but present to some extent in the utilitarians, that being moral is a matter of being kind, compassionate, and caring in our dealings with others: Moral interests are interests in the well-being of others. Third, there is the idea that morality requires us to be fair and impartial, to respect rights and to follow accepted rules in our dealings with others. This idea of impartiality also plays a role in utilitarianism and in Kant's theory, and the importance of rights and social rules is stressed by Hume and Hobbes.

It is this idea of fairness and impartiality, of doing one's part, of following rules, of respecting abstract rights and treating everyone alike, that is perhaps the most difficult to appreciate and to justify. Though what exactly will be best for us as individuals may be controversial ("do I really need to go to school?"), most of us at least would like to pursue our own best interest if we knew what it was. And just about everyone is moved by compassion and concern for some people. We don't want to hurt others if we can avoid it. But the demands of impartial morality, like the demands of justice, seem to require that we set aside these particular concerns. As Kant saw, and as even Hume admitted, compassion and benevolence can prompt us to act contrary to the requirements of fairness and justice. By the same token, if we think morality requires only kindness or concern for the interests of others, then we provide an easy justification for many things that seem to *violate* impartial morality. (Whom do I *hurt* if I cheat a little on an exam?) Because it is the most difficult to justify and to understand, I will devote a good part of this chapter to a modern account of these demands of impartial morality. The conception of morality I will describe is often called "contractualism." Contractualism is not the whole of morality, the only proper concern of ethics, but it is arguably an essential framework within which other aspects of ethics must play out their distinctive roles.

A DEMOCRATIC CONCEPTION OF MORALITY

In one of his attempts to describe the imperative of morality, Kant suggests that we think of the moral law as a law we make for ourselves, intending it to apply impartially both to ourselves and to everyone else. As moral agents, we should conceive of ourselves as sovereign legislators, making our own laws, but also subject to them. This democratic image is an attractive metaphor for at least a part of morality. It includes the idea that moral principles are principles we make for ourselves, for our own purposes. It also includes the idea that acting morally is a matter of impartially applying to oneself the same standards one applies in judging others. Both ideas are central to the contractualist conception of morality; and, accordingly, this conception can also be said to include the Kantian ideal of respect for persons as ends in themselves. When we act toward people in accordance with principles that we all can endorse from an impartial perspective, we treat them as ends, not merely as means. But this idea of principles impartially acceptable to all requires a good deal of further discussion.

The point of morality, on this contractualist conception, is different from the point of morality as conceived by, say, Aristotle or Epictetus. The point is not to make one's own life as good as possible. Rather, it is to provide principles that can serve as impartial, common standards to govern our interactions with others. Such standards, in turn, serve two purposes. First, as the aims of different people lead them into conflict, they can appeal to shared standards to resolve the conflicts. Second, as Hobbes and Hume emphasized, it is often true that all can gain if their interactions are coordinated by a common system of rules. Moral principles, then, function to adjudicate conflicting claims and also to define mutually beneficial schemes of cooperation.

The Kantian idea is that the rules serving these purposes are rules we "legislate" for ourselves to apply to all. As Kant pictures this idea, however, he usually imagines a single individual formulating rules to apply to everyone. Contractualism is even more explicitly democratic. According to contractualist theories, rules that serve the purposes I described should be rules that are acceptable to everyone--they are rules to which everyone could agree. Different people, of course, have different needs, interests, and commitments, and morality can be thought of as a system for adjudicating among them impartially. Contractualism interprets impartiality to mean that moral principles must take into account everyone's point of view; and it takes this to mean that they must be principles each could accept or agree to.

How could it happen that any individual might take an interest in moral principles, so conceived? Not everyone does. Some, when faced with conflicts, may be indifferent to whether the conflicts can be resolved by appeal to shared standards. They will simply do the best they can to get their own way. But I suspect such people are rare. Most, when faced with the demands of others, or when making demands themselves, want to be able to justify what they do to others whose interests are involved.[1] This, again, is part of what it might mean to treat others as ends, not means. Yet justification works only when there are principles for evaluating competing claims that are already agreed to or that others at least could be convinced to accept. Hence, for people motivated by the desire to be able to justify their conduct, there is reason to want principles that can gain the allegiance of others as well as oneself; but principles that can do that will have to be principles that people will not view as being biased. People who have the concept of justification to others and who care about being able to do so, then, will have an interest in discovering moral principles as these are conceived by contractualists.

The idea that impartial principles are principles everyone can agree to is a plausible idea; yet not every agreement guarantees impartiality, and so not every principle people might agree to at a given time is a principle to which we could expect people to give their continued allegiance. Not every agreement will continue to serve as a publicly acceptable common standpoint for adjudicating disputes. People might agree to something, at a given time, out of ignorance or confusion; they might agree to rules that are biased in favor of others because they were coerced or deceived into doing so; or they might agree just because others drove a hard bargain and they couldn't afford to hold out. Principles agreed to under such conditions are unlikely to reflect the interests of different people impartially. From a purely practical standpoint, the agreement is unlikely to remain stable. More important, those who seek impartial principles because they genuinely want to be able to justify their conduct to others in terms that others can reasonably accept will not be satisfied with principles agreed to in such circumstances.

Contractualist philosophers are moved by the ideal of being able to live with others in conditions of freedom and openness, secure in the knowledge that they can justify their conduct to others in terms that they can be expected to find acceptable. In practice, of course, we do not now have agreement on standards of conduct, much less agreement arrived at under conditions ensuring that the standards are impartial. In trying to formulate principles to resolve moral issues, then, contractualists have tended to think in terms of *ideal* agreements-- agreements arrived at under ideal conditions. The idea is to imagine what people would agree to if they were unbiased, were thinking clearly, were free from unfair pressures to compromise, and so on. Principles people would agree to under ideal circumstances will be fair and impartial. Though others may not now accept them, there is a decent chance that they can be led to do so. If we act on them, we act in the knowledge that we can defend what we do in terms that others at least could accept.

There is more than one way to develop this idea of an ideal agreement, and so more than one way to develop contractualist principles. An extremely influential version is due to John Rawls and is worked out in great detail in his book *A Theory of Justice*.[2] Rawls is not interested in moral principles in general, but only in the principles governing the design or reform of basic social institutions--the legal, political, and economic institutions of a society. But these are very important principles, for our shared institutions are a frequent focus of moral conflict. After all, they determine the basic framework within which we all live our lives. Rawls refers to such principles as "principles of justice," and his aim is to defend a particular conception of what they require.

Rawls's idea, like the general contractualist idea I have tried to describe, is that these principles should be principles everyone could find acceptable--principles to which everyone could agree. But Rawls does not think that principles everyone would agree to at a particular time, like today, would necessarily be good principles. They would be too much like a "mere" political compromise among interest groups, and they would reflect unfair distributions of power and wealth that already exist in society. Instead, he proposes the following account: Principles of justice are principles we would all agree to and commit to for the future if we were choosing on the basis of rational self-interest-- *if* we had also forgotten all of the distinguishing facts about ourselves. Thus, we are to imagine ourselves choosing as if we don't know whether we are black or white, male or female, from a rich or poor background, talented at music or math, etc. Rawls's thought is that principles agreed to by people in this situation will be fair and acceptable to any actual person, since people who don't know what their own situation is like will be careful that the rules don't disadvantage any type of person. (Imagine, for example, that people had to choose principles that will govern welfare policy or determine the permissibility of affirmative action, without knowing whether they are rich or poor, members of a majority or minority race.)

This is an attractive version of contractualism, yet it needs to be developed carefully. One question Rawls faced was how we could understand the idea of choosing principles at all if the choosers have forgotten what their needs, desires, and interests are. His answer was to assume that there are certain basic things anyone needs, and so he suggested that each would choose on the basis of a desire for as much of these as possible. But this raises several questions. For example, how can we be sure we have the right list of "basic goods"? And why should we think principles chosen in ignorance of many of our *particular* goals and interests will be satisfactory to us in our real lives, where these goals and interests may be more important to us than great amounts of basic goods? (What if I would prefer more protection for the environment and less money?)

Another question is whether what people would choose, in advance, on the basis of self-interest, will seem like a good choice later, even if they knew all their interests in advance. After all, a self-interested person may still be willing to take some risks (just as people sometimes choose to go without health insurance in the hope they won't need it). Yet what I would have chosen on the basis of self-interest may not seem like a good choice later. Rawls argues that a rational, self-interested person, faced with this fundamental choice, will choose cautiously; but some of his critics have disagreed. (Would I favor generous welfare provisions, on the chance I might be poor, or would I gamble that I would have a good job? Either way, does the fact that a self-interested person would choose a certain way, in advance, show that the principle chosen would actually be justifiable to those who had to live under it?)

Rawls's idea of moral principles as principles that would be chosen behind a "veil of ignorance" is a most attractive idea, and I have hardly done justice here to what, for him, is an elaborate and still-developing project. Nevertheless, the worry that what people *would* choose, in advance, on the basis of self-interest might not be something they would continue to find acceptable as their lives unfold is a real worry for a theory like Rawls's. More specifically, it is a worry for anyone who is attracted to the basic contractualist idea that what is morally required of us should depend, in some way, on what we can actually accept or on what can actually be justified to us. Accordingly, I will turn my attention to a different contractualist account of morality, one inspired by Rawls's work, but different in important respects.

This version is outlined in a recent article by T. M. Scanlon. Following a discussion of the general aims of theoretical moral philosophy, Scanlon offers a definition of what makes something morally *wrong*: "An act is wrong if its performance under the circumstances would be disallowed by any system of rules for the general regulation of behavior which no one can reasonably reject as a basis for informed, unforced general agreement."[3]

This is tricky. To find out whether an act is wrong, according to this definition,we have to go through two steps. We have to ask whether it violates a valid principle, but in order to decide whether a principle is valid, we have to ask whether anyone could reasonably reject that principle. Lots of people may object to the act, but that does not make it morally wrong. For it to be wrong, it has to violate a principle, and the only valid principles are those to which *no one* has a reasonable objection. (By defining what is wrong, Scanlon indirectly defines what is required: An act is required if it is wrong not to do it. Similarly, an act is permissible if it is not wrong.)

Scanlon speaks of rules no one can reject, instead of rules everyone can accept, because he suspects that some self-sacrificing persons *could* accept rules no one would consider morally obligatory. At the same time, we do not show that something is permissible just by showing that someone could reject a principle prohibiting it for *some* reason. The rejection must be *reasonable*, Scanlon says, and he means reasonable *given the aim of finding mutually agreeable rules* [111]. The thought is, roughly, that moral principles are principles that could be agreed to by everyone who is genuinely interested in finding a mutually acceptable system of moral principles. Moral principles are principles that could not be reasonably rejected by anyone who cares about morality. (This is an important qualification, and I will say more about it later.)

An upshot of this account of morality is that it is hard to show that something is wrong. The burden of proof, as it were, is on the moralist. To show that an act is wrong, one has to show that it violates rules that *no one* (given some interest in morality) can reasonably reject. That means that, if a requirement would impose a great burden on some people for no reason that could be made intelligible to them, then it is not a true moral requirement. It is a requirement they could "reasonably reject." Of course, their rejection has to be *reasonable*. For anyone who finds Scanlon's theory attractive, *the* crucial issue is how to explain when an objection to a rule is or is not reasonable. As Scanlon understands this idea, it would be unreasonable for me to reject a rule because it imposed a small burden on me if it was also the only way to secure a great benefit for others. Consider an example like drunk driving. There is, no doubt, some sacrifice involved in making a commitment not to drive drunk, but that does not mean that it is reasonable, for a person genuinely motivated to find mutually acceptable principles of conduct, to reject a rule against driving drunk. The sacrifice is small compared to the risk of death or serious injury for innocent people. Hence, there is a plausible contractualist argument that driving drunk is wrong.

Admittedly, this example is not totally uncontroversial. It essentially involves a comparison of benefits and burdens and, certainly, for some people it is genuinely hard to refrain from drinking and driving. To argue that drunk driving is wrong on contractualist grounds, one has to show that even if the sacrifice is hard to make, it is *worth* making in terms of the benefit of protecting life and limb. I think that is the right judgment, but I mention it to draw attention to the fact that some such judgment *has* to be made in the course of contractualist moral argument. What is distinctive about contractualism is not that it avoids judgments of relative value, but that it ensures that everyone's values at least get a hearing (and when a proposed moral principle imposes on someone a sacrifice that is not worth making, in terms of relative value of the benefits, then that person gets a veto).

Let me summarize this section. What a part of morality requires is that we act in a way that takes into account, impartially, the conflicting claims and interests of different persons; and this can be understood to mean that we must respect principles based on an impartial consideration of the interests of different persons. This part of morality calls on us to stand back from our own interests and from those of others close to us and evaluate our conduct from a perspective others can share. But those who care about living with others in conditions of openness and good faith, who want to be able to justify their conduct to others, will have a reason to seek and to act on principles acceptable from a standpoint like this.

But what principles are impartial ones? The basic contractualist idea is that impartial principles are those acceptable to everyone-- from every point of view. This is surely a plausible idea, and it fits nicely with the motive for being moral that I have just suggested: People will want to follow moral principles if they want to be able to justify their actions to others. This will be possible for anyone who follows principles acceptable to everyone.

There is a problem, however. In the world we know, there aren't many principles that everyone accepts. And even when there is, or might be, widespread agreement on principles, it often seems that people agree for the wrong reasons: They are ignorant of the facts, they are biased by "special interests," or they have given in too quickly to someone driving a hard bargain. In short, there is reason to doubt that actual agreement, even when it is achieved, is agreement on genuinely impartial principles. Hence, contractualist theory has been led to the idea that moral principles are principles people would agree to in ideal circumstances. We have considered two versions of this idea. First, we looked at Rawls's idea that principles of justice are principles people would choose, on the basis of rational self-interest, if they lacked knowledge of crucial facts about their own situation. Second, we considered Scanlon's idea that they are principles no one could reasonably reject, *given an interest in morality*--an interest in finding mutually agreeable standards of conduct. In each case, the qualifications seem necessary to ensure that the principles chosen really are impartial. Self-interested choosers who know their situation will seek to tailor principles to benefit themselves. Consequently, we need either to deprive them of knowledge, as Rawls does, or else allow them a "vote" only if they are motivated by something other than self-interest, as Scanlon does.

It is Scanlon's version that I will assume for the rest of this chapter. Before concluding this section, however, something more needs to be said about the motive for caring about morality, as conceived by contractualism. A motive for wanting to comply with impartial principles, it was suggested, might be the desire to be able to justify one's conduct to others. Moreover, if impartial principles are characterized as principles everyone could accept, it seems as if these are just the principles someone with this motive would want to follow.

If everyone can accept these principles, then, if I follow them, I can justify my conduct to anyone. But moral principles, as defined by both Rawls and Scanlon, are not principles *everyone* either does or even can accept. For Rawls, they are principles people would choose *in conditions of ignorance.* For Scanlon, they are principles people cannot reject, *given a desire to find mutually agreeable principles.* A desire to justify one's conduct to just anyone, in the actual conditions of the real world, then, will not automatically lead a person to want to follow contractualist principles. On the other hand, I wonder whether, on reflection, it should seem important to be able to justify oneself to just anyone. Perhaps it is enough to be prepared to justify ourselves to others who have a genuine interest in taking up the moral point of view. People who have this motive will have an interest in complying with Scanlon's principles, for these are just the principles such people cannot reject.

WHAT CONTRACTUALISM MIGHT REQUIRE

It is in the nature of contractualist morality that we can't say with certainty what it requires. Its requirements depend on what can be justified to people, and it is always possible that we have overlooked a legitimate objection to an alleged principle. Contractualism represents more an image of moral reasoning, an attitude toward morality and toward people, than a specific set of requirements. It tells us to examine moral demands in light of the way they both burden and benefit people. It tells us to examine both our principles and our conduct in terms of what we can expect to justify to other morally motivated people. Still, when we adopt this attitude, we can certainly make some plausible guesses about what would be required. Surely, for example, rules against most uses of violence, against killing, physical assault, and coercion would be parts of a contractualist morality. As the world is, it is little or no sacrifice, for practically anyone, to refrain from these things, and it is a great benefit for everyone to be protected from them. It is hard to see how these rules could reasonably be rejected. At the same time, however, contractualism suggests arguments for qualifying some of these rules. Exceptions in the case of self-defense, for example, seem like something people would insist on, and that does not seem unreasonable. Thus, it appears that many of our ordinary ideas about the wrongness of (most) acts of violence would be a part of contractualist morality.

Someone might object here that not everyone has reason to accept even rules against force and violence. Rich and powerful warlords, for example, can protect themselves from attack and may want to remain free to attack others. It is important to recall, though, that Scanlon regards moral principles not as principles no one can reject on the basis of self-interest. Instead, they are principles that can't be rejected by anyone already committed to the ideal of discovering and living under mutually acceptable principles. (And, similarly, in Rawls's approach to justifying moral principles, though people choose on the basis of self-interest, they don't know whether they have the power of Genghis Khan or whether they are poor peasants.)

In contractualist morality, arguments for some sort of property rules are also likely to succeed. As discussed above, in the chapter on Hume, stable property arrangements benefit us in many ways, both direct and indirect. In this case, though, unlike that of rules against violent assault, there is a lot of room for reasonable disagreement about some of the details of property arrangements, and it is likely that which ones are best will depend on local circumstances and needs. In addition, as in the case of traffic laws, it is on some points arbitrary just how the rules are formulated so long as they are well known and generally followed. (It doesn't matter whether we drive on the right or the left, as long as we drive on the same side.) Thus, it seems likely that no *particular* system of property rules would have the status of a basic moral requirement. Instead, it would be morally permissible for communities to develop conventional or legal rules of property. The only moral rules would be general requirements that, for example, whatever rules we adopt be generally fair and beneficial. Beyond that, all morality would say is that each person should comply with established local rules--again, assuming that these did not impose unfair burdens on individuals or groups.

The idea here, obviously, is like Hume's idea that the requirements of justice develop by convention. It contrasts with the idea, suggested by Kant's Universalization Principle, that we can always find out what is required by asking, in the abstract, "what if everyone did that?" If everyone *were* to drive on the left, after all, that would be fine. But, surely, what I should actually do depends on what other people are actually doing, that is, on the local conventions.

The contractualist idea about the role of conventions and institutional arrangements, though modeled on Hume's ideas, nevertheless does not follow Hume in all respects. For one thing, there is no claim that whatever conventions arise among self-interested persons are morally obligatory. There could well be contractualist principles putting limits on which conventions were even permissible. Thus, for example, property rules that permitted unlimited accumulations of wealth while others lived in poverty might be ruled out by principles no one could reasonably reject. Second, it is not built into contractualist morality that the requirements of morality can be identified with the requirements of benevolence--that what we should do, in general, is whatever promotes happiness or well-being. Indeed, as Hume himself saw, the idea that we ought to comply with conventional rules of property and contract means that we must sometimes do things that are harmful. And that means there is an awkward tension within Hume's overall theory. By contrast, in the contractualist theory outlined here, there could well be a direct requirement that we comply with fair and beneficial conventional rules. I will have more to say about this specific issue in the next section.

How might a contractualist approach a specific moral dispute? Recall the case, described in Chapter 3, of a dispute between an environmentalist and someone who wants to ride his motorcycle through mountain meadows. What the environmentalist claims is that the cyclist acts immorally. The cyclist disagrees. If the environmentalist is correct, that means, according to this conception of morality, that no one can reasonably reject a rule against riding motorcycles in these meadows. But the cyclist will object to this rule. So who is right? The question, of course, is whether it is *reasonable* to reject the rule. For contractualists, that is what the dispute comes down to.

One possibility, and I think this is an important consequence of contractualism as formulated here, is that *no* rule directly resolving this issue can gain universal assent. What that means is that both those who want motorcycles and those who want to use the meadows for quiet meditation are within their moral rights. But, at the same time, neither has a moral right to have it his or her own way. Both parties will have to get off their moral high-horses and try to work out a practical accommodation. (Morality might well permit a range of possible solutions.)

On the other hand, if there is some moral principle to resolve this dispute, it is likely to look something like a compromise. Whether it is reasonable for the motorcyclist to reject a rule against riding in the meadow will depend, for example, on just how the rule might be qualified. Moral discussion, as conceived by contractualists, is bound to involve the presentation of alternative rules, for the basic issue is going to be whether a proposed moral rule places unreasonably great burdens on some for the sake of insignificant benefits to others. One way burdens can be unreasonable is that there is another way to get the same benefits at lower cost.

I have suggested that contractualism involves as much an *attitude* toward moral issues as it does a specific resolution of those issues. That is the attitude I mean to be illustrating with this example. It tells us to approach issues of moral controversy in a spirit of openness, with respect for the interests and opinions of others, and to seek solutions that are reasonable from the perspective of all who are involved, and are willing to consider compromise. It rejects self-righteous dogmatism, for though it holds that there are morally right and wrong actions, it denies that moral rightness is something independent of what can be reasonably accepted by everyone who might be involved.

To make any moral argument, a contractualist must of course be prepared to offer and defend some idea of what it is or is not *reasonable* to reject. Any moral theory has its costs, and the cost of contractualism, in Scanlon's version, is the cost of spelling out this idea. Indeed, in a lot of moral arguments, this is what is likely to be the main point of controversy. Without getting into details, there are a couple of general points that need to be emphasized. First, for Scanlon, the issue is what is reasonable not from a purely self-interested point of view but from the point of view of those who have moral motives to begin with. Anyone who still thinks that egoism is our only possible motive will, of course, object to this idea; but we have seen that there is no good reason to make this assumption. It is certainly an idea that Aristotle rejects; and I take the arguments of Butler and Hume (Chapter 4) to show conclusively that it is false. People have aims other than their own self-interest, and there is no reason to think they are unwilling to consider the needs and interests of others in deciding what to accept or reject.

Second, however, it seems hard to deny that what men and women can reasonably reject depends on their own aims and concerns and, though people have aims that are not self-interested, their own good is certainly one of their important concerns. In the context of this book, this is especially interesting, for it is one of the points where the part of ethics on which Aristotle and Epictetus focused becomes relevant to contractualist theory. What can be reasonably rejected depends on how much it burdens some and how much it benefits others, but we can decide how great the relevant benefits and burdens are only in light of some conception of the good life. When we argue that a principle can reasonably be rejected, for example, we might claim that it requires some to sacrifice things essential to their good, while it secures for others things that may be nice but are far from necessary. It is not hard to see how it could make a difference, in arguments like this, whether we side with a Stoic like Epictetus or whether we side with someone closer to Aristotle.

PROBLEMS OF COLLECTIVE ACTION

Philosophers have observed that people in communities need to have and follow social rules of many kinds. They need to have systems of traffic rules determining who has the right-of-way at intersections. They need to have rules about how, and under what conditions, people can dispose of trash and other potential pollutants. And, as Hume especially noted, they need to have rules about property and contracts that specify how property is acquired, who has what property, and how people can engage in mutually beneficial transactions of various kinds. There is no doubt that we are all better off when rules of these various types are generally accepted and generally followed. They give people security, they protect public health and safety, they make life more predictable, and they do a great deal to make economic progress possible. Many philosophers, including Hobbes and Hume, have also thought it obvious that people are morally required to obey rules like these. Yet they have a difficult time explaining, in terms of their own assumptions, *why* people ought to obey them or *how* they could have adequate motives to do so.

The problem, as I argued in Chapter 4, is that the benefits of compliance with these rules, though very substantial, are often not much affected by what any one person does. Consider rules concerning the disposal of garbage and sewage. Small amounts of waste, if dumped in the river, will quickly disperse and cause no problem; yet if the whole community disposes of its wastes in this way, we have a public health disaster. Hence, we all benefit from having sanitation rules. But once they are in place and followed by virtually everyone, why shouldn't I violate them occasionally if it is more convenient or cheaper to do so? After all, this is like the original situation where the population is too small to do any damage.

The situation with property rules is often similar. If no one shoplifts, that helps to keep prices low for everyone. Stores don't have to employ security guards or pay for expensive electronic surveillance, and consumers don't have to mess with complicated, cumbersome packaging whose sole purpose is to make it hard to steal things. We all pay a big price for the fact that a lot of people do shoplift. But, if no one else is shoplifting, I can take a small item without causing all these problems and, indeed, probably without even causing a noticeable loss to the merchant I steal from. Moreover, even if a lot of other people are shoplifting, whether or not I do, at least on a particular occasion, may not make any noticeable difference. In this case then, as in the case of pollution, the good effects of compliance with the rules, or the bad effects of noncompliance, are largely independent of what any *one* of us, acting alone, chooses to do.

Now Hume, as I said in Chapter 4, certainly thinks people are morally required to obey what he calls "rules of justice and property." What is not clear is whether he can explain why this is so in terms of his own theory. In general, he thinks morality requires us to do what promotes happiness and well-being and to prevent pain and unhappiness. He thinks, moreover, that we have a certain amount of natural compassion and benevolence so that we are naturally motivated to do these things. The problem is, though, that complying with social rules, in particular cases, often does *not* serve to promote happiness or prevent unhappiness. Self-interest may tell us to disregard the rules in our own case, and benevolence may provide no counterweight to self-interest. Indeed, in some cases, benevolence may tell me to *violate* the rules. (Imagine someone who shoplifts to feed her hungry children, or someone who tells a friend, in danger of failing, what will be on the test.)

Hume was aware of these problems, but, in my judgment, he never solved them. Hobbes was also aware of them, and he was especially concerned with the problem of how people could be *motivated* to respect necessary social rules. His answer was that they could not be adequately motivated unless there was a strong, sovereign government enforcing the rules with coercive threats.

We have discussed this issue in connection with the theories of Hume and Hobbes, but it was not emphasized that it also presents a problem for utilitarian theory. Utilitarianism requires that we do whatever promotes the most net well-being--the greatest balance of happiness over unhappiness. But, if we look at issues like shoplifting and pollution from the perspective of this theory, it again appears that the theory may not say that these activities are wrong. Utilitarian *legislators* would no doubt favor *laws* against pollution and shoplifting. Their attitude might be much like Hobbes's. They might think people would comply with such laws only if they were forced to by the threat of criminal sanctions and so, since they would see great benefits to the community as a whole from these laws, they would establish such sanctions. (The reader will recall that Bentham, who sees people as purely self-interested, thinks we usually need "external sanctions" to get us to act as utilitarianism requires.) However, while utilitarian legislators would favor laws like these, their theory does not imply that it is morally wrong to violate them in particular cases. After all, utilitarianism requires us to do what will have the best consequences in the circumstances, taking into account the effects on everyone, including ourselves. Hence, if a little shoplifting will benefit me and my family, but will have negligible bad consequences for others, a consistent utilitarian can have no moral objection.

Several of the moral theories we have discussed, then, are unable to explain why it is wrong (assuming it is) not to do our part in complying with social rules that generally benefit society. Some people, of course, might not think this is a problem at all. They might say that it is just silly to follow rules in particular cases when doing so is unnecessary to bring about any good results. In particular, some utilitarian writers have thought it a good thing about their theory that it does not require "blind rule worship." Writers like Hume, on the other hand, were convinced that morality did require compliance with things like property rights. Another philosopher who probably would have agreed is Kant, and at least on the face of it, his theory seems better designed to explain why.

According to Kant's Universalization Principle, we should decide what to do by asking a question like "what if everyone did that?" If we apply this principle uncritically to questions like whether to shoplift, to dump wastes into the river, or to cheat on one's income tax, the principle clearly seems to say that we should do none of these things. After all, while my individual act of shoplifting may have negligible bad consequences, the consequences would be disastrous were everyone to do the same.

While theories like utilitarianism and Hume's theory tell us to focus on the consequences of our own acts, Kant's leads us to look at what would happen if people in general act as we propose to act. That is why Kant's theory seems to give a different answer to the shoplifting question and the pollution question. For someone who is convinced that shoplifting or cheating on taxes is always wrong, then, Kant's theory seems like a better theory than Hume's. And, quite apart from the mere accidents of what our parents may have told us, there are good reasons for thinking that people shouldn't pollute and shouldn't shoplift. At least it is clearly true that we all benefit from the existence of a system in which these kinds of behavior are minimized. Again, though, within some theories it is hard to see how we can have a good objection to any *particular* act of shoplifting or polluting, even though, taken together, a lot of such acts would be bad.

All this may sound like a good reason for accepting Kant's Universalization Principle and rejecting more utilitarian theories. However, there are also serious difficulties with Kant's principle. First, as we saw in Chapter 3, Kant's principle is ambiguous in the sense that it can give different results, depending on how the act under consideration is described. For example, suppose I say not that I am considering shoplifting but that I am considering "shoplifting-in-a-situation-in-which-no-one-else-is-shoplifting." It would *not* be bad if everyone did *that*, so, Kant's principle would not rule it out after all.

Perhaps someone will say that I am not being fair to Kant here, because Kant would insist that we describe acts in a way that doesn't bring in all sorts of specific details before we attempt to universalize them. But there is another problem with Kant's theory if we rule out including specific details in our act descriptions. Suppose we consider the case in which social cooperation has badly broken down. Almost no one is paying taxes, and most everyone is littering and spoiling the land and waters. This would be a bad situation, to be sure, but one might think--I think--that, in that case at least, we no longer have obligations to pay taxes or not to pollute. Yet, if we don't allow ourselves to mention the specific facts of the situation in the descriptions we universalize, Kant's principle seems to say that we must "cooperate," even if we are the only ones doing so. We must cooperate, just because if everyone does, the result is good, and if everyone doesn't, the result is awful.

The contractualist approach to moral reasoning has a better way of dealing with this issue, a way which avoids the problems of both the Humean/utilitarian approach and of Kant's Universalization Principle. According to contractualists, morality requires compliance with principles no one can reasonably reject, given the aim of finding mutually agreeable principles for regulating conduct. These principles, I have suggested, would *allow* people to enter into mutually beneficial conventions or to establish mutually beneficial institutional arrangements. They would also, I think, *require* us to comply with such conventions, once they were established. They would not tell us to make foolhardy (or heroic) sacrifices when no one else was willing to go along. We could all reasonably object to that requirement. But unlike principles that focus only on the actual good consequences our own actions produce, contractualist principles would tell us to do our part when a fair and effective cooperative arrangement was in place and functioning well. Why?

The benefits of cooperation--for example, of cooperation with rules against polluting--are available, obviously, only if most people do cooperate. Hence, everyone would certainly favor a principle that most everyone else cooperate with genuinely effective and beneficial arrangements. At the same time, assuming that everyone benefits, that the benefits are distributed fairly under the arrangement, and that no one is asked to shoulder an unfairly large burden, anyone could reasonably object to a moral principle requiring cooperation from him, but not from all others who benefit. Hence, even though a few people could fail to cooperate without any significant bad consequences, no principle *allowing* people to "free-ride" could gain the acceptance of all. The fact that widespread cooperation is needed by everyone, together with the fact that any principle requiring cooperation must be justifiable to each, yields the result that *universal* cooperation is morally required. Again, though--and here the theory borrows more from Hume than from Kant--what is actually required of any actual person will depend on what conventional or institutional rules have developed and are functioning effectively in one's own community.

I am claiming that a principle requiring that we do our part in mutually beneficial cooperative arrangements can be defended by a contractualist argument. This is the kind of principle that has come to be called "the principle of fairness,"[4] and it has been the subject of a good deal of controversy in the philosophical literature. I believe it can be defended, but only in a carefully qualified form. Thus, for example, only those who actually benefit more than they are asked to contribute are obligated to cooperate, and then only if they receive a fair share of the benefits. But given that these conditions are satisfied, and that other people are themselves accepting burdens, then those others have a right to the cooperation of the rest of the beneficiaries. These beneficiaries have an obligation to do their part. For example, if we have a community association that hires people to take care of community parks and assesses dues from everyone on a fair basis, then if you and everyone else pay your dues, you have a right to expect me to pay mine--unless, for some reason, my dues are set too high, or I am excluded from the park or don't in any way benefit from it. (One interesting thing about this principle is that if it does become widely accepted in a community, it constitutes a reason for following itself! For general compliance with this principle is itself a mutually beneficial practice.)

I mentioned above Hobbes's idea that people cannot be expected to comply with social rules unless there is a government enforcing the rules with threats of punishment for noncompliance. All I have argued so far is that contractualist morality would include a principle explaining why it is wrong not to cooperate with mutually beneficial rules. I have not tried to argue that people would necessarily, in particular cases, have sufficient rational motives to comply with that rule (or, for that matter, with any other part of contractualist morality). That takes us back to the question "why be moral?" and I will return to it at the end of the chapter. I should say here, however, that there is reason to agree with Hobbes, at least to an extent. We do not need to assume people are bad, selfish, or generally indifferent to morality to see that coercion may be needed to secure compliance with cooperative social arrangements. Even if people generally are willing to do their part, they may well not want to if they think others won't do theirs. Indeed, according to the principle of fairness, if others don't cooperate, we aren't required to cooperate either. What coercion can do is to give each of us some assurance that we are not simply being fools if we do our part. Without such assurance, even well-meaning people might not have good reason to cooperate.

Coercion by itself, on the other hand, probably cannot guarantee adequate compliance. No police force is that efficient; and if Hobbes thinks otherwise, he is probably wrong. Still, for the reasons given, coercion may be necessary. But that leaves us with the question of whether coercive institutions that punish people for failing to cooperate with social rules are morally permissible. In contractualist morality, that is the question of whether penal institutions would be prohibited by rules no one could reasonably reject. I suspect the answer is "no." Individuals would, I assume, insist on safeguards protecting them against arbitrary arrest, protecting the innocent from unjust sanctions, and prohibiting excessive or cruel punishments. But, given the facts of the world, including those mentioned in the previous paragraph, people could reasonably object to a blanket prohibition on the government's use of coercion.

Morality, as conceived here, would require cooperation with all sorts of beneficial social rules, and it would prohibit many uses of force or violence against others; but there is also a lot it would permit. It would leave individuals free to pursue personal projects and goals, within the bounds of respect for the rights of others, and it would also permit the establishment of institutional arrangements, including (suitably regulated) coercive penal institutions. Where restrictions will benefit everyone, without unreasonable cost, they will become moral restrictions. But, where it is possible to sustain substantial and reasonable objections to a proposed restriction, it will not become a part of morality. As individuals, and as a society, contractualist morality leaves us with a good deal of moral liberty.

CONTRACTUALISM AND UTILITARIANISM

These two very different approaches to moral theory nevertheless have some features in common. Both agree, for example, that popular moral beliefs about particular issues should be subjected to critical scrutiny. Such popular beliefs may reflect nothing more than the accidents of upbringing, and perhaps class ideology or prejudice as well. And both theories agree in rejecting appeals to authority as a way of resolving disputes. For each, what we ought to do depends on what courses of action can be justified by appeal to good reasons; and both share the humanistic idea that good reasons are reasons that refer to people's needs, interests, and purposes. In short, according to both, the requirements of morality, if any, are requirements that serve human purposes.

Some utilitarians, I believe, take the fact that utilitarianism opposes dogmatically asserted, purposeless requirements as a sufficient reason for being a utilitarian. Bentham argued that way: If we reject an uncritical reliance on what we happen to believe and also reject the principle of asceticism (which requires us to promote pain and suffering), he thought we were left with utilitarianism as the only alternative. But contractualism *agrees* with utilitarianism in its insistence that morality serve good purposes, yet it gives a very different picture of what morality is all about, and it yields different moral requirements.

In Mill's attempted proof of the principle of utility, what he actually attempts to show is that happiness is the good for people. This is not an idea that contractualists need to reject, though, like Aristotle, they may well think it does not get us very far. (The important question, as Aristotle emphasized, is the question of what happiness consists of.) But, while contractualists can agree with Mill "that each person's happiness is a good to that person," they need not go on to conclude, as Mill does, that "the general happiness" is "a good to the aggregate of all persons" [Mill, 34]. The contractualist need not say, as Bentham does, that "the interest of the community," conceived as "the sum of the interests of the several members who compose it," is the standard by which conduct is to be assessed as right or wrong [Bentham, 2-3].

Contractualists who agree that each person's happiness is good for that person do not see that fact as the solution to the problems of morality. Rather, they see it as a source of moral problems. My happiness may be good for me, and yours for you, but this may lead us into conflict. What makes me happy may make you unhappy, and vice versa. Utilitarianism says we should simply do whatever produces the larger amount of happiness. But suppose you will enjoy your preferred alternative more than I will enjoy mine. Why should *I* think that a good reason to give up mine? Perhaps, if I am feeling generous, I would be willing to; but, even then, why should I feel that I morally *must* do so? Yet that is what utilitarianism says, and that is where contractualism disagrees.

Contractualism begins with the idea that each person wants to lead a happy life and to realize various other personal goals and values. It recognizes, however, that none of us can live and pursue these goals in isolation from the others. This generates both problems and opportunities. On the one hand, it leads to conflict and controversy, and thus to demands for a principled way of settling disputes. At the same time, it offers the possibility of cooperation for mutual advantage in those cases in which we can all better our lot by coordinating our behavior. Given both these facts, the best practical response for each (at least for those who have some interest in being able to justify their conduct to others) is to try to identify a system of rules we all can accept, establishing our individual rights and furthering mutually beneficial cooperation. Morality is conceived as a system of rules which people who accept this idea and who want such a system of rules could not reasonably reject. Contractualists do not assume that these rules will require maximization of total happiness or well-being. They do not even assume that people will think this idea makes sense. Rather, morality is a system of rules under which individual people can reasonably expect to achieve decent lives for themselves in an atmosphere of mutual forbearance and cooperation.

In describing utilitarianism, Mill emphasizes that it can require very substantial sacrifice. A full-fledged commitment to the principle of utility, he says at one point, would require "a feeling of unity with our fellow creatures" of a kind which, he thinks, "Christ intended" [Mill, 26]. This remark of Mill's makes sense, it seems to me, when we reflect on the fact that utilitarianism tells us to maximize total happiness, regardless of whose happiness it is and regardless of the cost in terms of reduced happiness, that it may be necessary for others to bear. Contractualism, by contrast, focuses not on the total sum of happiness but, rather, on what can be justified to the various, distinct individuals who may be affected by what we do. Accordingly, it tends to endorse courses of action that are compatible, so far as possible, with the good of each; and it encourages us especially to mitigate the bad consequences of what we do on those who might be left worst off.

Still, it would be a mistake to think that contractualism endorses anything like pure self-interest. Certainly, it requires us to submit to a system of mutual forbearances and to cooperate with mutually beneficial rules, even when this involves some cost in terms of our own interests. Neither does contractualism, as described here, assume that moral principles are somehow based on or derived from purely self-interested choices. Contractualist principles are not conceived as principles that purely self-interested bargainers would agree to. (Morality is not like a negotiated bargain between, say, a used car dealer and a potential purchaser, each motivated solely by a desire to maximize personal financial advantage.) Instead, it is like an agreement among persons, each of whom wants *mutually* advantageous rules, rules that others will find satisfactory as well. For in contractualism, each is viewed as having a higher-order desire to be able to live with others in relations of mutual respect, where that means, at least, that each wants to identify standards of conduct which, if followed, will enable each to be able to justify his or her conduct to others in terms that the others will find satisfactory. If that is what it is like to treat others as ends, not merely as means, then respect for contractualist morality amounts to respect for a fundamental injunction of Kantian morality.

ARISTOTELIAN AND HUMEAN THEMES

Ethical theories that differ from one another are not necessarily in conflict, because not all ethical theories mean to answer the same questions. Contractualism and utilitarianism probably do conflict, since each is an attempt to say what is required when conduct is assessed from a social or impartial point of view. They are attempts to say what structure of rights and duties should govern interactions between people. A theory like Aristotle's, by contrast, is concerned mainly with what kind of life is best from the point of view of the person who lives it. A theory like Aristotle's complements utilitarianism and contactualism more than it conflicts with them.

In my discussion of Mill, I observed that he adopts a conception of happiness a good deal like Aristotle's. I also remarked above on one way in which contractualism and Aristotle's theory are related: To justify a moral judgment, a contractualist must claim that certain principles can or cannot be reasonably rejected by persons seeking mutually acceptable principles for the regulation of their conduct. To show that, one needs to make a judgment about the impact of proposed principles on the well-being of individuals. But someone who accepts contractualism as the correct story about our basic rights and duties toward one another can perfectly well think Aristotle was right about the nature of the good life for an individual. The two are perfectly compatible and, indeed, complementary.

In fact, an Aristotelian theory of the good may be more congenial than other conceptions to contractualist morality. For Aristotle does not identify one's good with whatever one *happens* to want. Hence, a conflict of actual desires does not mean that there are no principles compatible with the good of each. Moreover, for Aristotle, individual good does not depend too much on the kinds of goods that are likely to be in scarce supply.

Aristotle did not deny completely the need for scarce "external goods" or the desirability of "goods of fortune." Still, for Aristotle, human good consists most importantly not of what one has, but of what one does--of the exercise of developed skills and abilities. Aristotle himself tended to emphasize a rather narrow range of intellectual skills and activities. He thought the life of a philosopher was the best possible human life. But I have expressed doubt about this particular claim. Still, it does seem to me plausible that, for each of us, a good and satisfying life will probably consist in part of the active exercise of skills and abilities in tasks which, *for us*, are fairly challenging and therefore absorbing. Whether this is playing baseball, managing a household, singing in a choir, or building model airplanes will depend on our particular interests and abilities.

For contractualists, this is an attractive idea, for the hope of contractualism is that there are rules that promote the good of all in a way compatible with the good of each. Yet, as Hume noted in his discussion of justice, this approach requires that what each needs is not so scarce that there is no possibility of moral arrangements that are compatible with the good of each. On an Aristotelian view, while each needs some goods of the type that may be scarce (e.g., food, shelter, money), no one needs too much, and most of what gives us the greatest satisfaction is our own activities and our own projects--things that are not in short supply at all.

Now I want to turn to another connection between Aristotle's theory and contractualism. Aristotle claimed that certain moral virtues-- excellences of character--contribute to one's ability to live a good and happy life. Given the rest of what he says about happiness, this claim seems plausible for a good number of the virtues he mentions. For example, it is easy to see how temperance frees us from distractions and discomfort that would otherwise interfere with the activities in which we develop our skills and abilities. However, as I suggested in my chapter on Aristotle, it is less clear how to show that people need the virtue of justice. Moreover, within Aristotle's theory, which proceeds from the perspective of a single individual concerned with living a good life, it is hard to see how one could produce and justify any particular account of what justice requires.

Justice has to do with our interactions with one another. It has to do with what we owe to others, with their rights, and, more generally, with the proper distribution of benefits and burdens. And these are matters that must be settled from some standpoint independent of the standpoint of any particular individual. Contractualism proposes such a standpoint. It proposes that we seek an account of our respective rights and duties by asking, roughly, what general rules and conventions would be acceptable to each. Assuming there are some such rules, and assuming they specify a system of rights and duties and determine how benefits and burdens are to be distributed, then contractualism can give an account of the content of the requirements of justice. Thus, while Aristotle's theory offers an account of the good that helps to fill out the notion of "reasonableness" required by contractualist theory, contractualism can produce an account of the content of the virtue of justice that Aristotle needs.

Contractualism, like other modern moral theories, provides a way to determine what justice requires and, in that sense, supplements Aristotle's theory. The question remains, though, whether the virtue of justice, understood as the desire or disposition to comply with requirements of justice, is actually good for a person, as Aristotle thought. The answer, of course, depends both on what the good consists of and on what justice requires. Suppose we agree with Aristotle that friendship is an important good, and suppose we accept a contractualist account of moral requirements like justice. In that case, I believe we can make a plausible case that the virtue of justice is good for a person.

Friendship requires that we establish with others relations of trust, and that requires openness, honesty, and good faith. But only when we undertake to live with others on terms that all can freely and reasonably accept do we free ourselves from any need to coerce, manipulate, or deceive. At the most general level, what contractualist morality requires is that we undertake to live in just that way. It enjoins that we seek, with others, a way of relating that neither can reasonably reject--that both can freely accept. It denies that the good of anyone is to be subordinated to that of any other. When sacrifice is necessary, it requires that it be on terms both could agree to. In complying with contractualist principles, then, we can be confident that our conduct is justifiable to others who might be our friends.

Contractualism provides an account of an important part of morality. It by no means covers the whole of what ethics has traditionally been concerned with. Contractualism tells us to identify and comply with principles no one can reasonably reject. These will likely include prohibitions on (most) uses of force, violence, and deceit; they will include requirements that we come to the aid of those in danger and share with those in need; and they will include requirements that we comply with fair and mutually beneficial social conventions, like systems of property and contract and schemes of cooperation securing public goods, when these are widely respected and functioning effectively. And most of us do comply with requirements like these, most of the time, without giving it a second thought.

There are exceptions, of course. People steal. People certainly balk at paying their income tax, and many people probably cheat a bit at the margin, though paying taxes can often be construed as an example of contributing one's share to a mutually beneficial cooperative enterprise. And some full-fledged sociopaths live their whole lives by deceit and manipulation (though such lives are often short). Still, for the vast majority of us, the kinds of requirement that no one can reasonably reject represent only the minimal core of morality or, to vary the metaphor, only the framework within which we live out the real substance of our lives. I do not mean to minimize its importance. When we respect one anothers' rights, we respect the conditions within which it is possible to move on to establish bonds of mutual trust and friendship. Yet respecting rights itself remains, in crucial ways, minimal.

It is one thing to respect the rights of others and to act only within one's own rights. It is something else to exercise one's own rights *well.* Rights--property rights, for example--give a person a great deal of freedom. The freedom is not unlimited. I can't use my property in ways that violate the rights of others. But I still have a huge amount of choice as to how I use the property I have; and the same is true for my other rights. A system of rights and obligations no one can reasonably reject will likely leave each person with enough "moral space" to identify and lead a happy life. Whether we do lead happy lives, though, will depend on how we exercise our rights. A theory of the good life, like Aristotle's, is partly a theory about *how* we should exercise them, to the extent that we are concerned with our own good.

Whether we exercise our rights successfully, with respect to our own well-being, is not necessarily the only issue, however. There are at least two further points. First, as philosophers like Hume and Butler would insist, a part of morality might be identified with the demands of our own generous or benevolent nature. To the extent that we agree with this view--that we see kindness, compassion, and charity as moral impulses--it will be possible to get either good or bad moral marks for the way we choose to exercise our rights--for what we do even when we act within the constraints of contractualist principles. We can be kind and generous, or selfish and mean-spirited, either one, without violating the basic requirements of the contractualist framework; but morality, as conceived by Butler and Hume, says that we *ought* to be kind. Admittedly, as Hume saw, it is possible for kindness and compassion to *conflict* with rights (and that will make more sense if we see rights as a part of contractualist morality, with a foundation separate from benevolence). One possible view, and certainly the one that would be endorsed within the contractualist perspective, is that moral virtues like compassion are properly practiced only within the limits set by principles no one can reject.

Some parts of traditional ethical theory, like the theory of individual well-being and the emphasis on ideals of kindness and benevolence, I suggest, can be seen as attempts to address the question of how people should exercise their rights within the framework of a neo-Kantian, contractualist morality of rights and obligations. Though of great importance, this latter part of morality falls far short of a complete account of how to live. The Aristotelian virtues, as well as those emphasized by writers like Butler and Hume, supplement this account; but there may well be more to be said, some of which is specific to particular communities and social situations.

Contractualist morality, I said, won't by itself determine just what rules of property or political arrangements we ought to have. Communities will develop these on their own, and contractualist principles will require us to comply with them when they are fair and effective. Just how effective a given legal, economic, and political system is, however, will probably depend both on the basic structure of rights and duties it contains and also on how people operating within it choose to exercise their rights. To take a mundane example, employees can do just what is minimally required ("working to rule"), or they can try to do a really good job. That is certainly true for teachers, health care professionals, or politicians. And what constitutes a really good job will depend on features of the local situation. (Thus, for example, a politician in a democratic system might just watch the opinion polls and vote so as to get reelected. In my opinion, though, the system will function well only if political leaders exercise good judgment about what we *should* do as a community and then convince their constituents, if necessary, to change their opinions.) In general, then, I suspect there will be skills or virtues, particular ideals, like ideals of professional conduct, that will be extremely important in the context of a particular society at a particular time.

CONCLUSION: MORALITY--WHAT'S IN IT FOR ME?

We cannot answer the question "why be moral?" in any form, without first saying what morality is, what it requires. I have stressed this idea since my Introduction. Indeed, if someone sees morality merely as a set of abstract requirements or laws, if all he or she can tell me is that they are the requirements of morality or that following them is *morally* good, I do not see any reason why I or anyone else should pay attention. If people have reasons to be moral, it is because morality performs some function which people, in turn, have some reason to care about.

In this chapter, I have sketched a complex picture of morality. Sometimes, being moral is a matter of being generous, charitable, or compassionate. It involves reaching out to others, offering help, and sharing. Sometimes, again, we give high marks--though we may not think of them as high *moral* marks--to people who do their jobs well, who are skillful and conscientious. We also value virtues like bravery, honesty, self-control, trustworthiness, fairness, and cooperativeness. We think it bad to be cowardly, foolhardy, self-indulgent, greedy, or lazy.

I mean to include these ways of behaving, these character traits, in my account of morality; but they have not been the main focus of this chapter. The main focus has been on the framework of basic limits, within which we practice the more particular virtues. Gratuitous violence, cruelty, murder, malicious deception, stealing, and cheating violate basic framework principles. There may not be many such rules, and there is certainly room for disagreement as to their exact content, but some such framework is of great importance. It is primarily this framework that might best be understood in contractualist terms. It consists of those rules which no one, given an interest in finding a mutually acceptable framework of this kind, could reasonably reject.

If we think of morality as having different aspects--of there being more than one dimension of moral assessment--then the question "why be moral?" can have different answers, corresponding to these different aspects. Suppose, for example, that the question is what reason people have to be kind or generous, to give others a helping hand, even when they don't stand to gain any particular benefit in return. The answer is that some people may not have any reason. At least, there is no *guarantee* that they will. There are people who are simply blind to the suffering of others, who are so wrapped up in themselves that they either don't see it or don't care about it. Most of us are sometimes a bit that way, though in extreme forms this kind of indifference is likely pathological. But total indifference, as Hume and Butler insisted, is surely rare. So, as a matter of fact, the vast majority of people have reason to be kind or generous, at least to some extent. The vast majority will respond, at least emotionally, to evidence that someone is in need of help. "What's in it for them" is, simply, the satisfaction of their altruistic desires.

This claim is limited. I stop short of saying that everyone has a reason to be moral, even in the restricted sense in which morality amounts, roughly, to kindness. Though I certainly believe--again following Hume and Butler--that just about everyone has at least some direct concern for the welfare of others, I know no good argument to show that everyone must have such a reason. I do not know any way to show that the requirement to be kind is categorically motivating--inescapable--in Kant's sense. More obviously, as people differ in the degree to which they care for others, they differ in the extent to which they have reason to be kind or generous.

There is a further respect in which my claim is limited. To the extent that we have the Humean motives of sympathy and benevolence, we have reasons to be kind and generous, but that, on the view sketched here, is not all there is to morality. I have viewed compassion and kindness as morally good traits within a more general framework of moral principles derived from contractualist assumptions. These principles define the boundaries of permissible conduct. They define basic rights of the person, and they require compliance with a fair and beneficial political constitution and respect for fair rights of property and contract. But, as philosophers like Kant and Hume would agree, kindness can actually lead us to *violate* basic contractualist principles. It certainly does not automatically give us a reason to comply with them. What could give us such a reason?

To begin with, just as motives of kindness or benevolence may not always lead us to comply with contractualist principles, so also an extensive, altruistic identification with the good of others is not necessary to produce compliance. Utilitarianism demands that we sacrifice our own interests if doing so would produce even slightly more happiness for people generally, and it is hard to see how we could have a reason to do this unless we were moved by extreme, disinterested benevolence. But, it seems clear, this sort of utilitarian requirement could be reasonably rejected and so would not figure in the contractualist moral view described in this chapter.

Morality, as conceived here, requires that we seek an accommodation with others, an accommodation in which we neither dominate by force nor are dominated. It assumes that we view our own interests and concerns as legitimate, but view others as having legitimate concerns too. Principles that no one can reasonably reject constitute such an accommodation. Men and women who care about being able to justify their conduct to others would have a reason to comply with such principles.[5] This is the kind of concern that could motivate an interest in morality as described in this chapter. Of course, if the desire to be able to justify one's acts is an overriding desire, it would provide a reason to comply with principles others accept, even if one didn't accept them oneself. But people who have this desire and *also* have a mature sense of their own worth and of the value of their own concerns and interests will not be so quick to give in to whatever demands others make. Such people will be willing to question the judgments of others when they can't be defended by mutually acceptable principles.

An interest in being able to justify what one does, rather than, for example, a benevolent concern to promote good consequences, is the kind of motive that is needed to explain compliance with contractualist principles. For these principles, like Hume's principles of justice and like principles Kant defends, reflect demands that may conflict with what produces good consequences. Yet it is not hard to explain how people come to have an interest in justifying their conduct. After all, we grow up with parents, older siblings, and teachers, all of whom make demands and reward or punish us according to whether we obey. This could be, and probably is for some, an utterly arbitrary, authoritarian process. In the worst cases, parents may punish, for example, even when children try hard and do their best. But in many cases, certainly, there is room to discuss whether the demands are reasonable, and children have a chance to offer justifications and excuses.

The relation between parents and young children is, of course, decidedly one-sided. Parents have all the power. But that changes as children grow and, in any case, children also deal with other children, and with them they are on a more or less equal footing. The asymmetrical arrangement in which one demands and the other merely acquiesces gradually gives way to relations based on negotiation, bargaining, and compromise. Indeed, conditions of relative equality probably foster the motive to find mutually agreeable principles in two ways. First, when we don't view ourselves as powerless, we are willing to make demands; but second, if others are not subordinate to us, we will limit ourselves to demands that are not unreasonable from their point of view. And, as this happens, we move toward relationships governed by morality, rather than by force. Though demands no longer stem from arbitrary power, demands for justification and the felt need to meet them remain.

Attitudes like natural kindness and compassion, together with an acquired concern to be able to justify one's conduct to others, together provide us with reasons to be moral, as we have been describing morality. But these need not be the only reasons people have. In the first place, I have spoken as if kindness and the desire to justify always explain different kinds of moral action. Sometimes this is so, for sometimes respect for rights, say, actually runs contrary to instincts of kindness. Yet, of course, the two often coincide. Respect for my rights is usually good for me, too, and it usually involves no serious cost for others. Second, as Butler would have urged, any person's actual motives are extremely complex and varied. There is no reason why people might not have, or acquire, numerous specific desires that would reinforce the basic ones I have identified in providing motives for morality.

An example is the motive John Rawls has called "the sense of justice."[6] Rawls argues, among other things, that in mutually beneficial cooperative arrangements people who benefit will normally acquire, as it were, a sort of basic attachment to the principles underlying the arrangement. This attachment will manifest itself as a direct desire to do one's fair share, regardless of whether, in the circumstances, one's own contribution is strictly necessary. Thus, for example, people would acquire a basic desire to vote or to contribute to a charity they favor, even when their own contribution is negligible. This is not the place to go into details, but it is certainly true that people *do* make such contributions, even "when no one is watching." And I have said that contractualist morality would require cooperation in such arrangements. If Rawls is right about the sense of justice, then many people will have an additional motive for complying with these requirements.

A basic question remains. While it is a matter of some delicacy to say exactly what motives would provide reasons for compliance with the different kinds of moral requirement, it seems clear that most people can and do have such motives. In one sense, then, it is clear that people have reasons to be moral. Moreover, short of brainwashing, we are simply stuck with them. But is it to our advantage that we have them? Even without brainwashing, this is not a purely theoretical question, for, while we adults are the way we are, those of us who have children, and who care about them, may be able to do something about what kinds of motive they grow up with.

Here we come almost full circle, to the kind of question Aristotle asked. What role do the moral virtues play in the good life and, in particular, is it good for a person to have the virtue of justice? Suppose we take the virtue of justice to amount to a disposition to comply with principles no one can reasonably reject and to do one's part in fair and mutually beneficial cooperative endeavors. Is it good for a person to have motives to do these things? We have touched on this question in earlier chapters. It is not difficult to argue that others have a reasonable interest in how we behave, and that friendship will flourish only among those who are willing to cooperate and who take an interest in whether they can justify their conduct toward one another.

I have made this point before, and it suggests that it is good for us to take an interest in the justifiability of our own conduct. It is also worth saying, though, that friends worth having will be friends who do not make unreasonable demands. And the demands of morality, as understood here, are meant to be like the demands of a good friend.

Contractualism requires compliance with principles no one can reasonably reject. Those principles can certainly demand some sacrifice from us, for it is not reasonable to reject requirements that impose some burden if they also secure significant benefits for others and there is no feasible alternative. But sometimes there are feasible alternatives that impose even smaller costs for the same benefits. And sometimes other people demand large sacrifices for the sake of benefits that are small, uncertain, or controversial. Those demands can reasonably be rejected. If we understand the virtue of justice as the disposition to act as contractualism requires, then this virtue most certainly does not involve subordination of our own interests either to abstract rules or to the interests and needs of others. It requires that we pay attention to reasonable demands, and it requires that we seek a reasonable accommodation with others, but it does not require self-denial. It invites us to be open and frank about our own interests. In a sense that Kant might have found satisfactory, it requires us to follow just those requirements we can will, consistent with a decent respect for others and for ourselves.

NOTES

CHAPTER 1

1. Epictetus, *The Handbook of Epictetus,* trans. Nicholas P. White (Indianapolis: Hackett, 1983). Otherwise unidentified section references in the text are to this edition.

2. I first encountered this distinction in Anthony Kenny, "Happiness," *Proceedings of the Aristotelian Society,* New Series LXVI (1965-1966): 93-102.

CHAPTER 2

1. Aristotle, *Nicomachean Ethics,* trans. Terence Irwin (Indianapolis: Hackett, 1983). In referring to the text, I use either the conventional book and chapter numbers (e.g., Bk. i, Ch. 2) or, where more precision is called for, the page, column, and line numbers found in the margins of this edition and in most scholarly editions of the text: "1094a, 1" refers to line 1, column a of page 1094 in the standard Greek edition.

2. I borrow here from Gilbert Ryle's paper "Pleasure," *Proceedings of the Aristotelian Society,* Supplementary Volume XXVIII (1954): 135-146.

3. On this point, and in the next couple of paragraphs, I follow Philippa Foot, *Virtues and Vices* (Berkeley: University of California Press, 1978): 128f.

CHAPTER 3

1. Immanuel Kant, *Grounding for the Metaphysics of Morals,* 1785, trans. James W. Ellington (Indianapolis: Hackett, 1981). I rely on this translation, but my page references will be to the standard Prussian Academy edition of Kant's works. These appear in the margins of Ellington's edition and of most other scholarly editions of Kant's work.

2. David Hume, *A Treatise of Human Nature,* 1739, 1740, ed. L. A. Selby-Bigge (Oxford: Oxford University Press, 1888): 415.

3. In putting the issue this way, I am influenced by Philippa Foot, *Virtues and Vices* (Berkeley: University of California Press, 1978): 157-173; and by Bernard Williams, *Ethics and the Limits of Philosophy* (Cambridge, MA: Harvard University Press, 1985): 23f.

4. The role of these concerns in making the virtues good for us is something Philippa Foot has stressed in her writings. See *Virtues and Vices*, 129, 165-166.

CHAPTER 4

1. David Hume, *An Enquiry Concerning the Principles of Morals*, 1751, ed. J. B. Schneewind (Indianapolis: Hackett, 1983). Otherwise unidentified references to Hume will be to this edition.
2. David Hume, *A Treatise of Human Nature*, 1739, 1740, ed. L. A. Selby-Bigge (Oxford: Oxford University Press, 1888).
3. John Rawls, *A Theory of Justice* (Cambridge, MA: Harvard University Press, 1971): 126.
4. Joseph Butler, *Five Sermons*, 1726, ed. Stephen L. Darwall (Indianapolis: Hackett, 1983). References in the text to Butler are to this edition.
5. Thomas Hobbes, *Leviathan*, 1651, ed. Herbert W. Schneider (Indianapolis: Bobbs-Merrill, 1958). References in the text to Hobbes are to this edition.

CHAPTER 5

1. Jeremy Bentham, *The Principles of Morals and Legislation*, 1789 (New York: Hafner, 1948). References in the text to Bentham are to this edition.
2. John Stuart Mill, *Utilitarianism*, 1861, ed. George Sher (Indianapolis: Hackett, 1979). All references to Mill in the text are to the Hackett edition.
3. Peter Singer, "Famine, Affluence and Morality," *Philosophy and Public Affairs* 1 (1972): 229-243.

CHAPTER 6

1. This is the motive for being moral suggested by T. M. Scanlon in "Contractualism and Utilitarianism," in A. K. Sen and B. Williams, eds., *Utilitarianism and Beyond* (New York: Cambridge University Press, 1982): 116. I will describe Scanlon's own version of contractualism later in this section, and I will stress his account of the motive to be moral in my concluding remarks at the end of the chapter.
2. John Rawls, *A Theory of Justice* (Cambridge, MA: Harvard University Press, 1971).
3. T. M. Scanlon, "Contractualism and Utilitarianism," 110.
4. See John Rawls, *A Theory of Justice*, 342f.
5. This is the motive for moral behavior proposed by Scanlon and introduced at the beginning of my discussion of contractualism above.
6. Rawls, *A Theory of Justice*, Ch. VIII, esp. 472f.

SELECTED FURTHER READINGS

GENERAL WORKS

The Encyclopedia of Philosophy. New York: Macmillan, 1967.

>This is an excellent reference work for philosophy students. It includes good articles on all of the philosophers discussed here as well as on specific topics in ethics.

Larmore, Charles E. *Patterns of Moral Complexity.* New York: Cambridge University Press, 1987.

>A concise book that defends a pluralistic account of morality drawing on a wide range of historical texts and emphasizing Aristotle and Kant. Like contractualists, Larmore stresses issues of social morality and the importance of liberal, "framework" principles.

MacIntyre, Alasdair. *A Short History of Ethics.* New York: Macmillan, 1966.
Williams, Bernard. *Ethics and the Limits of Philosophy.* Cambridge, MA: Harvard University Press, 1985.

>These historical introductions to moral philosophy, like mine, stress differences between Greek ethics and the moral philosophy of the modern period. I present a more sympathetic account of the modern tradition than Williams does.

Nietzsche, Friedrich. *The Genealogy of Morals*, 1887. In *The Birth of Tragedy and the Genealogy of Morals*, trans. Francis Golffing. New York: Doubleday (Anchor), 1956.

>Writing in the nineteenth century, Friedrich Nietzsche criticized morality, arguing that it stems from weakness, represses our natural impulses, and that we do far better for ourselves if we can rise above morality and moral ways of thinking.

THE GREEK TRADITION

Cooper, John. *Reason and Human Good in Aristotle.* Cambridge, MA:
    Harvard University Press, 1975.

> An introduction to Aristotle's *Ethics,* focusing especially on the account of
> the good or happy life. For serious students.

Falk, W. D. "Morality, Self and Others." In *Ought, Reasons and Morality.*
    Ithaca, NY: Cornell University Press, 1986.

> An important paper setting out some of the differences between morality
> as conceived by someone like Aristotle and by philosophers in the modern
> tradition (e.g., Kant).

Kenny, Anthony. "Happiness," *Proceedings of the Aristotelian Society,* New
    Series LXVI (1965-1966): 93-102. Reprinted in Joel Feinberg, ed., *Moral
    Concepts.* New York: Oxford University Press, 1969.

> This article is mainly a discussion of two possible interpretations of
> Aristotle's *Ethics,* but it also draws a distinction between happiness as
> "contentment" and happiness as "richness of life," a distinction that has
> influenced my thinking about Aristotle and about the Stoics.

Foot, Philippa. *Virtues and Vices.* Berkeley: University of California Press,
    1978. (On Aristotelian ethics, see especially "Virtues and Vices," pp. 1-18,
    and "Moral Beliefs," pp. 110-131. I will mention other essays later, where
    relevant.)
Pincoffs, Edmund. *Quandaries and Virtues.* Lawrence, KS: University of
    Kansas Press, 1986.
Wallace, James. *Virtues and Vices.* Ithaca, NY: Cornell University Press, 1978.

> These three books are contemporary works in moral philosophy based on
> a more or less Aristotelian theory of the virtues.

MODERN MORAL PHILOSOPHY

Kant

Aune, Bruce. *Kant's Theory of Morals.* Princeton, NJ: Princeton University
    Press, 1979.

> An overview (which is not too detailed) of Kant's moral theory, including a
> commentary on the *Grounding* (which was the basis for my Chapter 3).

Foot, Philippa. "Morality as a System of Hypothetical Imperatives." Pages 157-
    173, in *Virtues and Vices.* Berkeley: University of California Press, 1978.

This paper is partly a critique of Kant's attempts to show that everyone necessarily has a reason to act on the categorical imperative, and it also defends the more general claim that, while moral people have reasons to be moral, there is no guarantee that *everyone* does.

Darwall, Stephen. *Impartial Reason*. Ithaca, NY: Cornell University Press, 1983.
Nagel, Thomas. *The Possibility of Altruism*. New York: Oxford University Press, 1970.

Two advanced and difficult books that attempt to defend, in the style of modern philosophy, the Kantian idea that it is irrational not to be moved by the demands of morality.

Nell, Onora. *Acting on Principle: An Essay on Kantian Ethics*. New York: Columbia University Press, 1975.

Attempts to demonstrate that Kant's categorical imperative can be interpreted so as to give clear and definite results.

Hume, Hobbes, and Butler

Campbell, Richmond and Lanning Sowden, eds. *Paradoxes of Rationality and Cooperation*. Vancouver, BC: University of British Columbia Press, 1985.

A selection of advanced readings on problems of social cooperation and collective action typified by the Prisoner's Dilemma.

Feinberg, Joel. "Psychological Egoism," Pages 489-500, in Joel Feinberg, ed., *Reason & Responsibility*. 7th edn., Belmont, CA: Wadsworth, 1989.

Offers an argument against the egoist thesis that people always act only in their own self-interest. His argument parallels, and supplements, the arguments found in Butler and Hume.

Foot, Philippa. "Euthanasia." Pages 33-61, in *Virtues and Vices*. Berkeley: University of California Press, 1978.

In the context of a lively discussion of "mercy killing" and related issues in medical ethics, Foot describes some clear examples of the tension between the demands of charity and the need to respect rights. She cites Hume's remarks on conflicts between justice and benevolence.

Gauthier, David. "Morality and Advantage," *Philosophical Review* LXXXVI, 4 (October 1967): 460-475.

Gauthier (who has also written a good book on Hobbes) argues that morality is beneficial for moral people, but only *indirectly*, in much the same way Hume and Hobbes think political institutions and conventions of justice benefit us indirectly: While we are all better off if we all comply, it may not be to the advantage of a particular individual to comply in a particular case. (This article includes a brief discussion of the Prisoners' Dilemma which I discussed in Chapter 4.)

Mackie, John. *Hume's Moral Theory.* London: Routledge & Kegan Paul, 1980.

Includes brief discussions of Hume's predecessors, including Hobbes and Butler.

Stroud, Barry. *Hume.* London: Routledge & Kegan Paul, 1977.

An interpretation of Hume's whole philosophy. Chapter IX, "Morality and Society" (pp. 193-218), is a good overview of the moral theory.

Utilitarianism and Contractualism

Hill, Thomas E., Jr. "Kantian Constructivism in Ethics," *Ethics* 99, 4 (July 1989): 752-770.

Discusses similarities and differences between contractualism of Rawls's kind and Kant's ethical theory. Explores the idea that contractualism provides an interpretation of Kant.

Mill, John Stuart. *On Liberty.* 1859. Elizabeth Rapaport, ed. Indianapolis: Hackett, 1978.

Rawls, John. *A Theory of Justice.* Cambridge, MA: Harvard University Press, 1971.

A long and difficult but extremely influential work in political philosophy. Rawls employs a version of the idea of the social contract as a way of defending certain moral principles for evaluating social and political institutions. Rawls's work was instrumental in the development of a new interest in contractualist thinking in ethics.

Ryan, Alan, ed. *John Stuart Mill and Jeremy Bentham: Utilitarianism and Other Essays.* New York: Viking/Penguin, 1987.

A good selection of various works by Mill and Bentham, together with a useful introduction by the editor.

Sidgwick, Henry. *The Methods of Ethics,* 1907. New York: Dover, 1966.

Includes in Book IV (esp. Chaps. I & II) one of the earliest really clear, modern formulations of utilitarianism. Sidgwick also offers an excellent account of the relations between utilitarianism and egoism, of the possible justifications for utilitarianism, and the limits of these justifications.

Smart, J.J.C., and Bernard Williams. *Utilitarianism, For and Against*. New York: Cambridge University Press, 1973.

An influential modern discussion of utilitarianism, in the form of extended essays by a well-known critic and a staunch defender.

ABOUT THE BOOK
AND AUTHOR

How are the demands of morality related to the needs, interests, and projects of people? Are they a burden, or are they good for us? Are they nothing but arbitrary impositions, or should we expect them to be justified? And will the answers to these questions tell us why and whether we should be moral?

In this short, accessible text, William Nelson poses these questions in a form appropriate for beginning students and treats them in a way that both they and their teachers will appreciate. In the company of major figures from the history of ethics, Nelson explores the key issues surrounding topics like egoism, altruism, the good life, and the requirements of morality. A special strength of his presentation is the way he demonstrates how the views of these historical figures prefigure the theories espoused by different schools of contemporary thought. Students get not only the historical positions in terms of which contemporary debates are framed but also up-to-date discussions of utilitarianism, contractualism, problems of collective action, and the relations between virtue and duty-based theories.

Nelson's own view that morality is not a single subject matter enables him to show how each of the historical traditions has a role to play in a coherent and defensible pluralistic account of morality. At the core of this pluralism is a commitment to the democratic view that morality must not merely serve practical human purposes, but it must also be justified to the people it governs.

Imaginative and insightful, intelligent and informed, this is an excellent first text for students of ethics and the history of ethics.

William N. Nelson is professor of philosophy at the University of Houston. He is the author of *On Justifying Democracy* and many articles and reviews on ethics and political philosophy.

INDEX